FIVE MODERN NŌ PLAYS

FIVE MODERN NŌ PLAYS

TRANSLATED FROM THE JAPANESE BY DONALD KEENE

BY YUKIO MISHIMA

Vintage Books

A Division of Random House
New York

FIRST VINTAGE BOOKS EDITION, April 1973

 Published in the United States by Random House, Inc., New York, and simultaneously in Canada by McClelland & Stewart Limited. Originally published in Japan as *Kindai Nōgakushū*. This edition originally published by Alfred A. Knopf, Inc., in 1957.

Library of Congress Cataloging in Publication Data
Mishima, Yukio, pseud.
Five modern nō plays.
Translation of Kindai nōgakushū.
I. Title.
[PL833.I7K513 1973] 895.6'2'5 72-8029
ISBN 0-394-71883-6

Manufactured in the United States of America

THIS TRANSLATION IS OFFERED
IN FRIENDSHIP AND GRATITUDE
TO *FAUBION* AND *SANTHA*

❁ *INTRODUCTION*

❁ *ONE OF* the first non-Japanese ever to see a Nō play was Ulysses S. Grant. In 1879 he stopped in Tokyo on a good-will journey around the world, and his hosts, rather at a loss what to offer in the way of entertainment to the rare visitor from abroad, asked the great Nō actor Hōshō Kurō to perform. It would not have been altogether surprising if the grizzled old ex-soldier had fallen asleep as he watched the solemn, hieratic movements of this subtle and symbolic art. It is recorded instead that after the performance he turned to his hosts in admiration and declared: "You must preserve this."

Grant probably did not know that it was a real question at the time whether or not the Nō would survive. It had been associated intimately since its creation in the fourteenth century with the Shogunate government, which was finally overthrown in 1868, and for that reason if no other it had fallen into marked disfavor with the victorious enemies of the old regime. This was, moreover, an age when Western things were frantically being imported and adapted into Japanese life. It appeared inevitable that a dramatic art which in 1879 was distinctly an archaic survival should have been one of the first victims of modernization. The fashionable people of the day, far from patronizing the Nō, flocked at night to the celebrated Rokumei Hall to dance to the strains of the waltz or to display their mastery over the mysteries of the knife and the fork. It seemed indeed that the future of the art was in peril. But Grant urged that it be preserved, and the recommendations of so distinguished a visitor were not lightly to be dismissed in those days of uncritical respect for all things foreign. Other support came from Japanese who, when traveling abroad, had witnessed performances of opera, and had concluded that since Nō rather resembled the opera it might be worth saving. The few Nō actors who had persevered in their art during the years of neglect gradually began to win audiences again, and gifts from the court and the nobility ensured that this unique dramatic form would continue.

Nō was preserved, but it was not free from the danger of turning into a kind of museum exhibit, to be accorded, like the operas of Monteverdi, pious and infrequent revivals. Certainly there was no great popular appeal in the Nō. It had been supported largely by the court of the Shogun, the military ruler of Japan, and it had steadily grown farther and farther away from the ordinary public. With the rise in the sixteenth century of the puppet theater and the Kabuki, dramatic forms with a broader appeal, Nō had become almost exclusively a court entertainment. Only infrequently were benefit performances open to the public. The court spectators were connoisseurs able to detect the slightest variation—good or bad—from the usual stage movements or sounds. The traditions were so strong that Nō tended to become almost a ritual, and so well versed in the texts were the audiences that it was unnecessary and even undesirable to make the plays dramatically convincing. The dialogue was pronounced in a deliberately muffled manner, and the gestures became completely stylized. A hand slowly lifted to the face denoted weeping, the stamp of a foot might mean a ghost had disappeared. That Grant should have been impressed by this remote and difficult art is little short of astonishing.

Nō originally was much simpler. It stemmed from various playlets performed at temples and shrines as part of harvest and other celebrations, or whenever the people of a village happened to congregate. In the fourteenth century this rustic entertainment was developed by the genius of two men, a father and son, into one of the world's great dramatic forms. These men were Kan'ami Kiyotsugu (1333-84) and Zeami Motokiyo (1363-1443). As established by them, only four or five actors normally appear in a Nō play: the principal speaker-dancer, a personage (often a priest) who does not dance, and various accompanying figures. The climax of each play is an extended dance which occurs near the end, and toward which the text from the outset has pointed. The plays themselves are seldom as long as a single act of a Western work, but a Nō drama requires about an hour to perform because of the final dance and the deliberate manner of recitation. There is a chorus and a musical accompaniment consisting of a flute and several kinds of drums, which serve to heighten moments of intensity.

In some respects Nō suggests ancient Greek drama: there are few characters; there is a chorus, dances, and masks (worn by the principal dancer in many cases), and an abundant use of traditional or legendary themes. However, unlike Greek drama, which became increasingly realistic, Nō developed into an essentially symbolic theater, where both the texts of the plays and the gestures of the actors were intended to suggest unspoken, indefinable realities. Some of the surviving works by Kan'ami indicate that in his day Nō was closer to European drama in that it was representational, but Zeami and his successors wrote plays in which the relation of the expressed part to the whole is like that of the visible surface to the entire iceberg. Zeami himself wrote a good deal on symbolism in the Nō. He believed that Nō should attempt through beautiful movements and words to point at an indefinable and limitless world beyond them. The nature of this world would depend both on the capacities of the actor to suggest and of the audience to comprehend.

Nō plays are usually divided into two sections. Often in the first part a character appears as an old woman, a fisherman, a reaper, or some other humble person, but in the second part the same character returns in his true appearance as a great warrior or a beautiful woman. Frequently we have to do with a ghost, a tormented spirit who asks to be prayed for, or one whose dreadful wrath must be exorcised. The world of the dead was perhaps uniquely suited to the peculiarly remote, symbolic nature of Nō, and the separation between life and death, the dead and the living, has never been more touchingly depicted than in Nō.

Once the form had been evolved and brought to its highest perfection by Zeami, Nō underwent few important changes. A seventeenth-century Nō play, in much the same way as one written in the fourteenth century, was likely to begin with a priest on a journey to some holy spot. There he meets a person of the vicinity whose strangely poetic words belie his humble appearance. The priest questions the unknown reaper or fishergirl, who gradually reveals the story of his former glory, and leads us to understand that some unsatisfied attachment to the world has kept his spirit behind. At the end of the play a hope of salvation, of deliverance from the attachment, is offered, and the ghost fades away. This was a typical form, and it enabled a playwright to give in a very abbreviated compass a poetic and complicated story. The reluctance of Japanese dramatists to abandon it is understandable. Nō plays continued to be written, but all the good ones of the sixteenth century and afterward when put together would not bulk as large as the work of Zeami alone. In the seventeenth century the puppet theater became the outlet for the dramatic genius of the country. It is not to be wondered at that Nō was forsaken by later dramatists: European composers did not go on writing madrigals when once the golden age had passed, and only seldom today does a composer choose to write for the harpsichord in preference to the potentially more expressive piano.

Yet Nō has continued from time to time to attract leading Japanese writers. Some have fashioned pastiches on the traditional themes, others have tried to fit modern conceptions into the old forms. The hysteria of wartime propaganda even led to the composition of a Nō play about life on a submarine. Some modern works have enjoyed temporary popularity, but they were essentially curiosities, having neither the beauty of language and mood of the old plays, nor the complexity of character delineation we expect of a modern work.

The first genuinely successful modern Nō plays have been those by Yukio Mishima. Indeed, we may say that if the medium is given a new lease of life it will be because of Mishima and his work. Despite his youth—he was born in 1925—Mishima is a man of exceptional breadth of knowledge, and he has drawn freely on both Japanese and Western sources in writing his novels and plays. His brilliantly successful novel *The Sound of Waves,* for example, had its genesis in the ancient Greek romance *Daphnis and Chloe,* and another novel concludes with a scene obviously suggested by Maupassant's *La Maison Tellier.* Some of Mishima's plays are on entirely modern themes, others in the style and language of the seventeenth-century Kabuki, and there is even a puppet play in the traditional idiom which is based on Racine's *Phèdre.*

Mishima seems to have been attracted both by the structure and the subject matter of the Nō plays. His adaptations have, of course, been free, for it has been his intent that these plays be wholly intelligible and completely contemporary. He has in fact suggested that if these modern Nō plays are performed in the United States, the adaptation should be carried one step farther. For example, the park where we first see Komachi gathering cigarette butts should be Central Park in New York, and for the Rokumei Hall, Delmonico's or some other famous spot should be substituted. There is no reason why so violent an adaptation cannot be made with complete success, and there is no question but that these plays have in their own right an immediate and powerful appeal even to people who are normally indifferent to Japanese drama.

The five plays of the collection were written between 1950 and 1955. They have been presented as modern plays on the Tokyo stage. *The Damask Drum* was performed in 1955 in traditional Nō style. *The Lady Aoi* was sung in 1956 as a Western-style opera.

Mishima's use of the original Nō dramas varies from play to play. Sometimes he has chosen only the general themes, at other times he has followed even the details of the originals. For example, the old man of the original *Damask Drum* who sweeps the garden of a palace becomes in the modern version a janitor who sweeps a law office in downtown Tokyo. The latter falls in love not with a princess but with the client of a fashionable couturière in the building across the way. In both versions the old man is told that he will win the favor of his beloved if he succeeds in beating a drum loud enough for her to hear it; in both cases the covering of the drum is damask instead of skin, and the drum makes no sound. The janitor, like the gardener, commits suicide. The Nō ghost returns to torment the cruel princess with the ceaseless beating of the drum, but in the modern play the lady's inability to love makes her deaf to the beating of the drum, and the janitor's ghost is driven a second time to despair.

Kantan follows the same story as the Nō progenitor. A traveler naps on a magic pillow, and during the brief time that it takes his hostess at the inn to cook a bowl of gruel, he dreams out a glorious life as Emperor of China. He awakens to the realization that life is but a dream. In Mishima's play, instead of a traveler, we have a spoiled young man of today who sleeps on the magic pillow while his old nurse prepares breakfast. His dreams are naturally not of ancient China but of riches and power as a financial tycoon and a dictator.

In *Sotoba Komachi,* Mishima has replaced the priests who dispute with Komachi by a poet. The priests are angry to discover Komachi sitting on a stupa (a *sotoba*), "the holy image of the Buddha's incarnation." The poet in Mishima's play berates Komachi for sitting on a park bench at night, when lovers want to be left alone. The main theme of the play, the story of the heartless beauty, Komachi, who refuses to yield to a lover unless he comes to visit her a hundred nights, is followed in Mishima's version. Here the poet asks the old hag about her life eighty years before, and gradually he finds himself re-enacting the part of her old lover on the hundredth night. The original Komachi was offered at the end of the play a promise of salvation, but the modern Komachi is at the end as she was at the beginning, a miserable old woman counting her nightly haul of cigarette butts.

In *The Lady Aoi,* a nurse in a modern hospital who talks not of demons but of sexual repressions is the counterpart of the priest who exorcises the living phantasm of Rokujō. Prince Genji, the husband of Aoi, who does not figure in the Nō play, appears in Mishima's as Hikaru: Hikaru, "The Shining One," had been an epithet of the dazzling Genji. The carriage in which Rokujō and Aoi contested the place of preference at the Kamo Festival becomes here a sailboat on which Rokujō and Hikaru recall the memory of their first meetings.

Hanjo is the farthest removed from the original play, which is almost the only Nō drama that has a happy ending. Hanako, the mad girl, is restored to sanity by the appearance of the man who had once abandoned her. In the modern play Hanako does not recognize her lover when he finally comes, and she turns him away.

The world of the psychiatric hospital, of the law office, and of the public park certainly seems a far cry from the dreamlike realms of the Nō, but however free Mishima's use of the original material, the dramatic situations remain identical. What Mishima has done principally is to add a modern understanding to the situations and to explore possibilities only vaguely adumbrated in the fifteenth-century texts. In *The Damask Drum*, again, the trick of asking the old man to beat a soundless drum is the invention of a spiteful dancing-teacher. The others who abet him in the cruel joke are a self-important diplomat, a foolish young man, and the worldly proprietress of a dressmaking establishment, all of whom are given sharply defined personalities. In the original the act was little more than the whim of a moment.

Mishima's use of the dramatic themes of the past may be likened to similar practices of European and American dramatists, such as Cocteau's treatment of the Œdipus story in his *Infernal Machine,* or O'Neill's adaptation of the Oresteia for his *Mourning Becomes Electra,* or even Brecht's *Threepenny Opera,* a modern version of Gay's *Beggar's Opera.* In none of these instances is it necessary to be acquainted with the original play in order to appreciate the new one. Each stands on its own merit, but at the same time a knowledge of the earlier work adds a dimension and permits us to measure the workings of a modern intelligence against a familiar background. Sophocles would have been startled to discover that in Cocteau's play the Sphinx is in love with Œdipus and herself yields the answer to her riddle; this unexpected turn not only attracts us but assuages our modern curiosity. (Why else should Œdipus have been the first to supply the answer to the riddle?) Similarly, the original Nō play offers no explanation as to why the princess should have caused the old man to beat a damask drum. Inevitably we feel that the story makes better sense as told by Mishima, whose use of the old story is at once respectful and courageous.

Again, the conclusion to Zeami's *Hanjo* shows the exchange of the fans by which the separated lovers pledge to marry. This is much too abrupt for us today. We have not even been prepared for Hanako's regaining her sanity, and the whole change is effected in a single line though, to be sure, the dance which accompanies it helps to clarify the situation. In Mishima's play even the exchange of fans cannot shake Hanako out of the madness into which she has been plunged by Yoshio's desertion. We can imagine her continuing to go every day to the railway station to wait for a lover she has in fact rejected.

The nature of our response to these modernized Nō plays is bound to differ from our response to a performance of the traditional ones. We are, for one thing, far more intellectually absorbed. The plays have the wit and invention we expect from an extraordinarily gifted writer. Oddly enough, Mishima manages somehow to suggest much of the uncanny symbolic quality of the originals, even in the tawdry modern surroundings of a public park or a downtown office. The five plays all have powerful overtones which even the uninitiated can feel. Hanako and Jitsuko looking into a future of waiting and non-waiting; the sinister tinkle of the telephone by Aoi's sick-bed; the kaleidoscopic visions of Jirō as he sleeps on the magic pillow; the tortured ghost who cannot make his beloved hear the drum even when it actually sounds; the old woman left in grim loneliness: all these evoke much the same sensations as the ancient plays and suggest why Mishima should have turned to them and their particular themes after having written numerous entirely new works.

The Japanese may well congratulate themselves on having been able to preserve the Nō through the period of greatest danger to it, when Western things seemed on the point of overwhelming all the native traditions. There are today larger audiences than ever for Nō plays, and new theaters are being built in Tokyo, Kyoto, and other cities. Most encouraging of all, perhaps, is the fact that an outstanding young writer has devoted himself to this traditional dramatic art, and in so doing has created works of unusual and haunting beauty.

DONALD KEENE

❁ *CONTENTS*

SOTOBA KOMACHI

CHARACTERS:

OLD WOMAN

POET

MEN A, B, AND C

WOMEN A, B, AND C

POLICEMAN

DANCERS, LOVERS,

VAGRANTS, WAITERS

❁ *THE SET is in extremely vulgar and commonplace taste, rather in the manner of sets used in operettas.*

A corner of a park. Five benches grouped in a semicircle facing the audience. Lampposts, trees etc. suitably disposed. Black backdrop.

It is night. Five couples on the five benches are rapturously embracing.

A repulsive-looking OLD WOMAN *enters, picking up cigarette butts. She goes on collecting them in the area around the five couples, quite oblivious to their discomfort, finally making her way to the bench in the center, where she sits. A shabbily dressed young* POET *comes under the lamppost and, drunkenly propping his body against it, observes the* OLD WOMAN.

The couple on the center bench presently stand up in anger, with expressions of annoyance on their faces, and leave arm-in-arm. The OLD WOMAN, *taking sole possession of the bench, spreads out a sheet of newspaper and starts counting the butts she has gathered.*

OLD WOMAN

One and one make two, two and two make four. . . . (*She holds a stub up against the light and, determining that it is a fairly long one, goes to the couple at the left to ask for a light. She smokes for a while. When the cigarette burns down to a stub she grinds it out, throws it on the paper with the others, and begins to count again.*) One and one make two, two and two make four. . . .

POET

(*Comes up behind the* OLD WOMAN *and watches what she is doing.*)

OLD WOMAN

(*her eyes still looking down at the paper*) Want a smoke? I'll give you one if you want it. (*She chooses a rather long stub and hands it to him.*)

POET

Thanks. (*Takes out a match, lights the cigarette, and smokes.*)

OLD WOMAN

Is there something else? Have you got something to say to me?

POET

No, not especially.

OLD WOMAN

I know what you are. You're a poet. That's your business, isn't it?

POET

How well you know. Yes, I write poems once in a while. There's no doubt but I'm a poet. But that doesn't make it a business.

OLD WOMAN

Oh? You mean it's not a business unless your poems sell? (*She looks up at the young man's face for the first time.*) You're still young, aren't you? But you haven't much longer to live. The mark of death is on your face.

POET

(*not surprised*) What were you in former life—a physiognomist?

OLD WOMAN

Maybe. I've seen so many human faces I've become sick of them. . . . Sit down. You seem a little shaky on your feet.

POET

(*Sits; coughs.*) I'm drunk, that's why.

OLD WOMAN

Stupid. You should keep both feet planted firmly on the ground, at least as long as you're alive.
(*Silence.*)

POET

You know, there's something that bothers me so much I can't stand it any more. Why do you come here every night at the same time and drive away whoever's here by sitting yourself on a bench?

OLD WOMAN

Is this the bench you're complaining about? I don't suppose you can be a tramp. What do you want? Do you collect money from people who sit here?

POET

No, it's simply that the bench can't talk for itself, so I'm talking for it.

OLD WOMAN

(*turning her attention from him*) I'm not chasing anybody away. When I sit down they run away, that's all. Anyway, this bench is made for four people to sit on.

POET

But at night it's for the use of lovers! Every evening when I pass through this park and I see a couple on every bench, it makes me feel so wonderfully reassured. I go by on tiptoes. Even if I'm tired or, as it happens once in a while, even if I feel inspiration coming over me, and I want to sit down so I can collect my thoughts, I refrain, in deference to them. . . . And you, old lady, since when have you been coming here?

OLD WOMAN

Oh, I see now. This is your little area—your special preserve—where you do your business.

POET

My what?

OLD WOMAN

This is where you forage for things to put in your poems.

POET

Don't be absurd. The park, the lovers, the lamposts—do you think I'd use such vulgar material?

OLD WOMAN

In time it won't be vulgar. There's nothing that wasn't once vulgar. In time it'll change again.

POET

What extraordinary things you come out with. If that's the case, I ought to deliver an impassioned plea on behalf of the bench.

OLD WOMAN

How tiresome you are. All you can say is that my sitting here is an eyesore, isn't that it?

POET

No—it's a profanation!

OLD WOMAN

Young people really enjoy arguments.

POET

Listen to me. . . . I am just what I seem, a threepenny poet, without even a woman who'll look at me. But there's something I respect—the world as reflected in the eyes of young people who love each other, a hundred times more beautiful than what they actually see—that I respect. Look, they're not the least aware we're talking about them. They've climbed up high as the stars. You can see the glint of starlight under their eyes, next to the cheeks. . . . And this bench, this bench is a kind of ladder mounting to heaven, the highest lookout tower in the world, a glorious observation point. When a man sits here with his sweetheart he can see the lights of the cities halfway across the globe. But if (*climbs on the bench*) I stand here all by myself, I can't see a thing. . . . Oh, I do see something—lots of benches, somebody waving a flashlight—must be a policeman. A bonfire. Beggars crouching around the fire. The headlights of a car. They've passed each other now and are heading toward the tennis courts. What was that? A car full of flowers. Performers returning from a concert? Or a funeral procession? (*He gets down from the bench and sits.*) That's all I can see.

OLD WOMAN

What rubbish. Why in the world do you respect such things? It's that same silly nature of yours which makes you write sentimental poems that nobody will buy.

POET

And that's exactly why I never invade this bench. As long as you and I are occupying it, the bench is just so many dreary slats of wood, but if they sit here it can become a memory. It can become softer than a sofa, and warm with the sparks thrown off by living people. . . . When you sit here it becomes cold as a grave, like a bench put together out of slabs of tombstones. I can't bear that.

OLD WOMAN

You're young and inexperienced, you still haven't the eyes to see things. You say the benches where they sit, those snotty-faced shop clerks with their whores, are alive? Don't be silly. They're petting on their graves. Look, how deathly pale their faces look in the greenish street light that comes through the leaves. Their eyes are shut, the men and women both. Don't they look like corpses? They're dying as they make love. (*Sniffs around her.*) There's a smell of flowers, all right. The flowers in the park are very fragrant at night, just like those inside a coffin. Those lovers are all buried in the smell of the flowers, like so many dead men. You and I are the only live ones.

POET

(*Laughs.*) What a joke! You think you're more alive than they are?

OLD WOMAN

Of course I do. I'm ninety-nine years old, and look how healthy I am.

POET

Ninety-nine?

OLD WOMAN

(*turning her face into the light*) Take a good look.

POET

Horrible wrinkles!

(*Just then the man of the couple on the bench to the far right yawns.*)

WOMAN

What's the matter? What makes you so rude?

MAN

Come on, let's be going. We'll catch cold.

WOMAN

You *are* disagreeable. You must be very bored.

MAN

No, I just remembered something funny.

WOMAN

What is it?

MAN

I was wondering whether my hen would lay an egg tomorrow, and it suddenly began to worry me.

WOMAN

What's the meaning of *that*?

MAN

There isn't any meaning.

WOMAN

You and I are finished. That's what it means.

MAN

Oh—there goes the last streetcar. We'll have to hurry.

WOMAN

(*She rises and stares at the man.*) What awful taste you have in neckties!

(*The man does not answer. He hurries the woman along and they exit.*)

OLD WOMAN

At last—they've come back to life.

POET

The skyrockets have gone out. How can you say they've come back to life?

OLD WOMAN

I know what the face looks like of someone who's come back to life—I've seen it often enough. It wears an expression of horrible boredom, and that expression is what I like. . . . Long ago, when I was young, I never had the sensation of being alive unless my head was all awhirl. I only felt I was living when I forgot myself completely. Since then I have realized my mistake. When the world seems wonderful to live in, and the meanest little flower looks big as a dome, and flying doves sing as they go by with human voices . . . when, I mean, everyone in the whole world says "Good morning" joyously to everyone else, and things you've been searching for ten years turn up in the back of a cupboard, and every girl looks like an empress . . . when you feel as if roses are blooming on the dead rose trees, then—idiotic things like that happened to me once every ten days when I was young, but now when I think of it, I realize I was dying as it happened. . . . The worse the liquor, the quicker you get drunk. In the midst of my drunkenness, in the midst of those sentimental feelings and my tears, I was dying. . . . Since then, I've made it a rule not to drink. That's the secret of my long life.

POET

(*teasing her*) Oh! And tell me, old lady, what is your reason for living?

OLD WOMAN

My reason? Don't be ridiculous! Isn't the very fact of existing a reason in itself? I'm not a horse that runs because it wants a carrot. Horses, anyway, run because that's the way they're made.

POET

"Run, run, little horse, looking neither right nor left"?

OLD WOMAN

"Never moving once your eyes from your shadow's track."

POET

When the sun goes down the shadow grows long.

OLD WOMAN

The shadow gets crooked. It gets lost in the darkness of evening.

(*As they talk the lovers on the benches around them all exit.*)

POET

Old lady, let me ask you something. Who are you?

OLD WOMAN

Once I was a woman called Komachi.

POET

Who?

OLD WOMAN

All the men who said I was beautiful have died. Now I feel for sure that any man who says I am beautiful will die.

POET

(*Laughs.*) Well, I'm safe. I didn't meet you until you were ninety-nine.

OLD WOMAN

That's right, you're lucky. . . . But I suppose a fool like you thinks every beautiful woman gets ugly as soon as she grows old. Hah! That's a great mistake. A beautiful woman is always a beautiful woman. If I look ugly now, all it means is that I am an ugly beauty. After having been told so many times by everybody how lovely I looked, I have found it too much of a nuisance during the past seventy or eighty years to start thinking of myself as being anything but beautiful. I still see myself as a raving beauty.

POET

(*aside*) What a heavy burden it must be to have once been lovely. (*To the* OLD WOMAN.) I can understand how you feel. A man who's once gone to war reminisces about the war all the rest of his life. Of course you were beautiful. . . .

OLD WOMAN

(*stamping her foot*) *Was?* I still *am* beautiful.

POET

Yes, yes, I understand. Why don't you tell me something about the old days? Eighty years ago, or was it ninety? (*He counts on his fingers.*) Tell me what happened eighty years ago.

OLD WOMAN

Eighty years ago . . . I was nineteen. Captain Fukakusa —he was at Staff Headquarters—was courting me.

POET

Shall I pretend that I'm Captain what's-his-name?

OLD WOMAN

Don't flatter yourself. He was a hundred times the man you are. . . . Yes, I told him I would grant what he desired if he visited me a hundred times. It was on the hundredth night. There was a ball at the Rokumei Hall, and simply everybody was there. I had become a little fatigued with all the heat of the party, and I was resting myself a moment on a bench in the garden. . . .

(*A waltz melody, faint at first but gradually becoming louder, is heard. The black backdrop is drawn aside to reveal indistinctly the Rokumei Hall, a ballroom built in Victorian architecture. In the foreground is a garden. The set is painted rather like the backgrounds which photographers formerly used for their pictures.*)

OLD WOMAN

(*looking offstage*) See! All the most boring people of the day have come.

POET

Those splendid-looking ladies and gentlemen?

OLD WOMAN

Of course. Shall we dance a waltz together to keep up with the others?

POET

Waltz with you?

OLD WOMAN

You mustn't forget! You're Captain Fukakusa.

(*Three young couples wearing costumes of the 1880's enter waltzing. They move to where the two others are dancing. The waltz ends. Everyone gathers around the* OLD WOMAN.)

WOMAN A

Komachi—how pretty you are tonight!

WOMAN B

I envy you so. Where *do* you get your clothes? (*She fingers the* OLD WOMAN'S *filthy rags.*)

OLD WOMAN

I sent my measurements to Paris and they made it for me there.

WOMAN A AND B

Did you really?

WOMAN C

It's the only way. There's always something slightly crude about any dress made by a Japanese.

MAN A

One has no choice. One simply must wear imported clothes.

MAN B

Yes, that's true for men too. Did you notice the frock coat the Prime Minister is wearing tonight? It was made in London—the home of gentlemen's fashions.

(*The women chatting and laughing surround the* OLD WOMAN *and the* POET. *The three men sit on the end bench and talk.*)

MAN C

Komachi is certainly lovely.

MAN A

By moonlight even an old witch would look beautiful.

MAN B

Komachi is one woman you can't say that about. She looks beautiful even in broad daylight. And when you see her in the moonlight, she's an angel, an angel from heaven.

MAN A

She's not one to give in easily to any man. I suppose that's why there are so many amusing stories about her.

MAN B

(*using French words which he translates as he goes along*) She's a *pucelle,* a virgin, that is. It's what you might call *une histoire scandaleuse,* you know, a kind of scandal.

MAN C

Captain Fukakusa is head over heels in love with her. Do you see how pale and drawn his face is? He looks as if he hasn't eaten for a couple of days.

MAN A

He's given himself to writing poems to Komachi, to the utter neglect of his military duties. It's small wonder the other officers at Staff Headquarters turn up their noses at him.

MAN C

Isn't there a man among us with the self-assurance to woo and win Komachi?

MAN B

All I have is an *espoir*. A hope, that is.

MAN A

If there's such a thing as the *espoir* of a sardine, I have it too. Poor fish.

MAN C

Me too. (*He bursts into loud laughter.*) Ummm. The worst thing about wearing a belt is that you have to adjust it every time you eat. (*He lets his belt out one notch.* A *and* B *do likewise.*)

(TWO WAITERS *enter, one carrying a silver tray with cocktails and the other a tray covered with hors d'œuvres. All help themselves. The* POET *stares vacantly at the* OLD WOMAN. *The three women, glasses in their hands, seat themselves on the bench opposite the one where the men are sitting.*)

OLD WOMAN

(*Her voice is very youthful.*) I can hear a fountain somewhere, but I can't see it. It's odd—when I hear it this way it makes me feel as if a rainstorm were pounding far off in the distance.

MAN A

What a lovely voice. It's clear, like the voice of a fountain.

WOMAN A

It's a lesson in eloquence just to hear her talk to herself.

OLD WOMAN

(*turning to the background*) They're dancing! Shadows are moving over the windows, and the windows grow light and dark by turns with the shadows of the dance. So wonderfully peaceful—like the shadows cast by flames.

MAN B

Isn't her voice sensuous? It's a voice that sinks deep into your heart.

WOMAN B

It makes me feel odd, even though I'm a woman, to hear her talk.

OLD WOMAN

Oh, I heard a bell ring. The sound of a carriage and horses' hoofs. . . . Whose carriage would it be? None of the princes has come yet this evening, but that bell sounded like one princely families use. . . . How fragrant the trees are in the garden. It's a dark, sweet, penetrating perfume.

MAN C

Alongside Komachi other women are merely women.

WOMAN C

Oh, how perfectly dreadful. She's copied the color of her handbag from mine.

(*The first sounds of a waltz are heard. All return glasses to the tray carried by the waiter and begin to dance.* OLD WOMAN *and* POET *remain as before.*)

POET

(*as in a dream*) It's strange. . . .

OLD WOMAN

What's strange?

POET

Somehow, I . . .

OLD WOMAN

Please do try to say it. I know what you want to say before you've said it.

POET

(*with ardor*) You, you're so . . .

OLD WOMAN

Beautiful— That's what you intend to say, isn't it? You mustn't. If you say it, you won't have long to live! That's fair warning.

POET

But . . .

OLD WOMAN

If you value your life, be still.

POET

It really is strange. I wonder if this is what is meant by a miracle.

OLD WOMAN

(*Laughs.*) Are there such things as miracles in this day and age? Miracles, indeed! First of all, they're so vulgar.

POET

But your wrinkles . . .

OLD WOMAN

What? I have wrinkles?

POET

That's what I mean— I can't see even one.

OLD WOMAN

Naturally! Would any man call for a hundred nights on an old hag? . . . But enough of your fantasies! Let's dance. Please let us dance.

(*The two begin to dance.* THE WAITERS *leave. A fourth couple joins* A, B, *and* C *in the dance. Presently all four couples sit, each on one of the benches, and begin amorous whisperings.*)

OLD WOMAN

(*while dancing*) Are you tired?

POET

No.

OLD WOMAN

You don't look well.

POET

It's the way I always look.

OLD WOMAN

Is that meant as an answer?

POET

Tonight's the hundredth night.

OLD WOMAN

And yet . . .

POET

Yes?

OLD WOMAN

Why do you look so grim?
(*The* POET *suddenly stops dancing.*)

OLD WOMAN

What's the matter?

POET

It's nothing—I just felt a little dizzy.

OLD WOMAN

Shall we go inside?

POET

No, it's better here. It's so noisy inside.
(*They stand with hands joined and look around them.*)

OLD WOMAN

The music has stopped. It's the intermission. How quiet it becomes.

POET

Yes, there is only silence now.

OLD WOMAN

What are you thinking about?

POET

Nothing. Or rather, I was just thinking something very odd. I had a feeling that if you and I were to part now, in a hundred years . . . probably less than a hundred years, we would meet again.

OLD WOMAN

Where would we meet? In the grave, perhaps? In heaven or in hell? Yes—they're the most likely places.

POET

Oh-h—something just flashed through my mind. . . . Wait a moment, please. (*He shuts his eyes, opens them again.*) It's the same as here. I will meet you again in a place that's exactly the same as this one.

OLD WOMAN

A big garden, gas-lamps, benches, lovers . . .

POET

Everything will be exactly the same. But what I don't know is how you and I will have changed by then.

OLD WOMAN

I don't believe I'll grow old.

POET

It might be that I'll be the one who won't grow old.

OLD WOMAN

Eighty years from now . . . the world will have progressed a great deal, won't it?

POET

But only human beings really change. Even after eighty years a daisy will still be a daisy.

OLD WOMAN

I wonder if there'll be quiet gardens like this somewhere in Tokyo.

POET

Every garden will have gone to seed.

OLD WOMAN

The bird will be the happier in them.

POET

There will be all the moonlight you could ask for.

OLD WOMAN

And if you climb a tree and look around, you'll see the lights of the whole city, and it will be just as if you saw the lights of all the towns all over the world.

POET

When we meet after a hundred years, what shall we say to each other?

OLD WOMAN

"Sorry we haven't kept in touch," I suppose.
(*The two sit on the bench in the middle.*)

POET

You'll keep your promise without fail, won't you?

OLD WOMAN

My promise?

POET

The promise about the hundredth night.

OLD WOMAN

Do you doubt it? After all I've said?

POET

Yes, tonight, for certain, I'll have my desires granted. And what a strange, lonely, disheartening feeling it is. It's as if you've taken into your hands something you've wanted and yearned for a long, long time.

OLD WOMAN

That, for a man, must be the most frightening feeling of all.

POET

My dreams realized. . . . And perhaps one day I shall grow tired even of you. If I should tire of someone like you, my life after death would really be horrible. And how frightening the eternal months and days until I die. I should simply be bored.

OLD WOMAN

Then you should stop at this, now.

POET

I can't.

OLD WOMAN

It's foolish to force yourself to finish something that you really don't want.

POET

But it's quite the opposite of something I don't want. I'm happy. I feel as if I could soar into the sky, and at the same time I am curiously depressed.

OLD WOMAN

You're too eager.

POET

And would you be quite calm if I tired of you?

OLD WOMAN

Yes. It wouldn't matter to me in the least. Someone else would begin the hundred nights of courting me. I should not be bored.

POET

I had just as soon die now, at once. Such an occasion hardly ever comes even once in a lifetime, and if it is to come for me, it will be tonight.

OLD WOMAN

Please do not weary me with such nonsense.

POET

Tonight it will be. And if I should spend tonight in thoughtless pleasure, as I have with other women— I shudder at the thought.

OLD WOMAN

Man does not live simply in order to die.

POET

Nobody knows. Perhaps man dies in order to live.

OLD WOMAN

How commonplace. How dreadfully ordinary.

POET

Help me, please. What shall I do?

OLD WOMAN

Go ahead—you can only go ahead.

POET

Please listen to me. Within a few hours, within a few minutes, a moment which could not exist in the world will come. The sun will begin to shine in the middle of the night. A big ship, its sails swollen with the wind, will ride up through the middle of the streets. I used often to dream such dreams when I was a boy; I wonder why. A big sailing-ship entering the garden, the garden trees beginning to thunder like the sea, the yardarms covered with little birds perching. . . . I thought in the dream, I'm so happy, I feel as if my heart will stop beating for joy.

OLD WOMAN

Dear me, you must be drunk.

POET

Don't you believe me? Tonight, in a few minutes now, an impossible thing. . . .

OLD WOMAN

Impossible things cannot be.

POET

(*He stares at the* OLD WOMAN's *face, as if to stir up memories.*) And yet, it's strange, your face . . .

OLD WOMAN

(*aside*) If he finishes these words his life is ended. (*trying to prevent him from speaking*) What is strange? My face? Look. See how ugly it is, how full of wrinkles. Come, open your eyes wide.

POET

Wrinkles? Where are the wrinkles?

OLD WOMAN

(*lifting her garment and showing it to him*) Look. It's in tatters. (*thrusting it under the* POET's *nose*) A horrible smell, isn't it? It's full of lice! Look at this hand. See how it is shaking, like a hand set in wrinkles. The nails are repulsively long—look!

POET

A wonderful fragrance. The nails are the color of a begonia.

OLD WOMAN

(*opening her robe*) Look, look at my breasts mottled a filthy brown. A woman's breasts should not be like this. (*In exasperation, she seizes the* POET's *hand and presses it against her breasts.*) Feel! Feel! There's no milk here!

POET

(*in ecstasy*) Ah, your body!

OLD WOMAN

I'm ninety-nine years old. Wake up—open your eyes. Look at me well!

POET

(*stares at her awhile as though stunned*) Ah, I've remembered at last.

OLD WOMAN

(*overjoyed*) You've remembered?

POET

Yes. . . . that's right. You were an old woman of ninety-nine. You had horrible wrinkles, mucus dropped from your eyes, your clothing stank.

OLD WOMAN

(*stamping her foot*) *Had?* Don't you realize I have now?

POET

Strange . . . you have the cool eyes of a girl of twenty, you wear magnificent sweet-scented clothes. You are strange! You've become young again.

OLD WOMAN

Oh, don't say it. Haven't I told you what will happen if you say I'm beautiful?

POET

If I think something is beautiful, I must say it's beautiful, even if I die for it.

OLD WOMAN

What madness! No more, I beg you. What is this moment you've been talking about?

POET

I'll tell you.

OLD WOMAN

No, don't. Please don't.

POET

It has come now. The moment for which we've waited ninety-nine nights, ninety-nine years.

OLD WOMAN

Your eyes are shining. Stop it, stop it, please.

POET

I'll tell you, Komachi. (*He takes her hand; she trembles.*) You are beautiful, the most beautiful woman in the world. Your beauty will not fade, not in ten thousand years.

OLD WOMAN

You'll regret saying such things.

POET

Not I.

OLD WOMAN

You are an idiot. I can already see the mark of death between your eyebrows.

POET

I don't want to die.

OLD WOMAN

I tried so hard to stop you.

POET

My hands and feet have become cold. . . . I'll meet you again, I'm sure, in a hundred years, at the same place.

OLD WOMAN

A hundred years more to wait!
(*The* POET'S *breathing ceases and he dies. The black backdrop is drawn. The* OLD WOMAN *sits on the bench staring at the ground. Presently she begins picking up cigarette butts as if for want of anything better to do. While she does so, a* POLICEMAN *enters and wanders around the stage. He finds the corpse and bends over it.*)

POLICEMAN

Dead drunk again! What a damned nuisance you are! Come on, get on your feet! I'll bet your wife's waiting up for you. Go on home quickly and get to bed. . . . Or is he dead? Yes. . . . Old woman, did you see him fall? Were you here?

OLD WOMAN

(*lifting her head a little*) It seems to me it was quite a while ago.

POLICEMAN

His body's still warm.

OLD WOMAN

That proves he must have just stopped breathing.

POLICEMAN

That much I know without having to ask you. I was asking you when he came here.

OLD WOMAN

About half an hour ago, I suppose. He was drunk when he came and he started making advances to me.

POLICEMAN

Advances to you? Don't make me laugh.

OLD WOMAN

(*indignantly*) What's so funny about that? It's the most likely thing in the world.

POLICEMAN

I suppose you defended yourself properly?

OLD WOMAN

No, he was just a nuisance, and I didn't pay any attention. He stood talking to himself for a while and before I knew it he collapsed and fell to the ground. I thought he had gone to sleep.

POLICEMAN

(*shouting toward stage-left*) Hey, you over there! You're not allowed to build bonfires in the park! Come here. I've got something for you to do. (TWO VAGRANTS *enter.*) Help me to take this body to the station.
(THREE MEN *exit carrying the corpse.*)

OLD WOMAN

(*painstakingly arranging the cigarette butts*) One . . . and . . . one . . . make . . . two . . . two . . . and . . . two . . . make . . . four. One and one make two, two and two make four. . . .

CURTAIN

THE DAMASK DRUM

❀ *CHARACTERS:*

IWAKICHI, *an old janitor*

KAYOKO, *a girl of about 20, a clerk*

SHUNNOSUKE FUJIMA, *a teacher of Japanese dance*

TOYAMA, *a young man*

KANEKO, *a member of the Ministry of Foreign Affairs*

MADAME, *owner of a fashionable dressmaking establishment*

SHOP ASSISTANT, *a girl*

HANAKO TSUKIOKA

❁ *THE CENTER of the stage is a street between buildings. Windows and signboards face each other on the third floors of the buildings on either side.*

Stage-right is a third-floor law office. A musty-looking room. A room in good faith, a forthright room. There is a potted laurel tree.

Stage-left is a third-floor couturière. A room in the most modern style. A room in bad faith, a deceitful room. There is a large mirror.

Spring. Evening.

(*In the room to the right.*)

IWAKICHI

(*He is sweeping the room with a broom. He sweeps up to the window.*) Out of the way, out of the way. You act as if you're trying to protect the dirt around your feet.

KAYOKO

(*She takes a mirror from her cheap handbag and stands in the light applying a fresh coating of lipstick.*) Just a minute. I'll be finished in just one minute now. (IWAKICHI *pushes up* KAYOKO'S *skirt from behind with his broom.*) Oh-h-h—you're dreadful. Really. The old men these days are getting to be horrible lechers. (*She finally moves aside.*)

IWAKICHI

(*sweeping*) And what about the young ladies? A girl of nineteen or twenty looks better when her lips aren't covered with all the paint. I'll bet your boy friend thinks so too.

KAYOKO

(*glancing at her watch*) I can't afford expensive clothes. Lipstick's the best I can do. (*She looks at her watch again.*) Oh, I'm really sick of it. I wonder why he and I can't both get off from work at the same time. Heaven help me if I tried to kill time waiting for him anywhere outside the office. The first thing you know it'd cost money.

IWAKICHI

I've never once set foot in any of those fashionable drinking places. But they know my face in all the counter restaurants. If you want to know where the bean soup is good, just ask me. (*pointing at the desk*) Once I invited the boss and he said it was first rate. I couldn't have been more pleased if he'd praised the bean soup in my own house.

KAYOKO

Business has not been good for the boss lately.

IWAKICHI

There're too many laws. That's why there're more lawyers than anybody knows what to do with.

KAYOKO

I wonder—when he's got such a stylish place for an office.

IWAKICHI

The boss hates anything crooked. I'm sure of that. (*looking at a picture on the wall*) It bothers him even if that picture-frame is a quarter of an inch crooked. That's why I've decided to spend the rest of my days working for him.

KAYOKO

(*opening the window*) The wind's died down since evening.

IWAKICHI

(*approaching the window*) I can't stand that dusty wind that blows at the beginning of spring. . . . The calm of evening. Oh, there's a good smell coming from somewhere.

KAYOKO

It's from the Chinese restaurant on the ground floor.

IWAKICHI

The prices are too high for me.

KAYOKO

Look at the beautiful sunset. It's reflected in the windows of all the buildings.

IWAKICHI

Those are pigeons from the newspaper office. Look at them scatter. Now they've formed a circle again. . . .

KAYOKO

I'm glad you're in love too. It's made you young again.

IWAKICHI

Don't be silly. My love is a one-sided affair, not like yours.

KAYOKO

You're in love with a great lady whose name you don't even know.

IWAKICHI

She's the princess of the laurel, the tree that grows in the garden of the moon.

KAYOKO

(*pointing at the potted tree*) That's the tree you mean, isn't it? There's nothing so wonderful about a laurel.

IWAKICHI

Oh! I've forgotten to water my precious laurel. (*Exits.*)

KAYOKO

Isn't he the sly one? Running off to cover his embarrassment.

IWAKICHI

(*Enters with a watering-can.*) Laurel, I'm sorry I forgot to water you. One more effort now and you'll be covered with glossy leaves. (*As he waters the plant he strokes the leaves fondly.*) Poets often talk about hair glossy as leaves. . . .

KAYOKO

You still haven't got any answer?

IWAKICHI

Mmmm.

KAYOKO

I call that disgusting. It makes me sick. Not to have the decency to send you an answer. Nobody else but me would go on being your messenger. How many letters has it been? Thirty, isn't it? Today makes exactly thirty.

IWAKICHI

If you count in all the love letters I wrote without sending them, it'd make seventy more. For seventy days—every day I wrote her one and every day I burned it. That's what it was like before you were kind enough to take pity on me and become my postman. Let's see, that makes a total of . . . (*Thinks.*)

KAYOKO

A hundred, of course. Can't you count any more?

IWAKICHI

Unrequited love is a bitter thing.

KAYOKO

You haven't the sense to give up.

IWAKICHI

Sometimes I think I'll try to forget. But I know now that trying to forget is worse than being unable to. I mean, even if being unable to forget is painful in the same way, it's still better.

KAYOKO

How did you ever get into such a state, I wonder.
(*As she speaks a light is lit in the room to the left.*)

IWAKICHI

They've switched on the light. Every day at the same time . . . when this room dies that one comes to life again. And in the morning when this room returns to life, that one dies. . . . It was three months ago. I'd finished sweeping and I just happened to look at the room over there, with nothing particular on my mind. . . . Then I saw her for the first time. She came into the room with her maid. The Madame was showing her the way. . . . She was wearing a coat of some kind of golden fur, and when she took it off, her dress was all black. Her hat was black too. And her hair, of course, it was black, black as the night sky. If I tried to describe to you how beautiful her face was— It was like the moon, and everything around it was shining. . . . She said a few words, then she smiled. I trembled all over. . . . She smiled. . . . I stood behind the window staring at her until she went into the fitting-room. . . . That's when it began.

KAYOKO

But she's not all that beautiful. It's her clothes—they're exquisite.

IWAKICHI

Love's not that sort of thing. It's something that shines on the one you love from the mirror of your own ugliness.

KAYOKO

In that case, even I qualify.

IWAKICHI

There's nothing for you to worry about! You look like a great beauty to your boy friend.

KAYOKO

Does that mean there's a moon for every woman in the world?

IWAKICHI

Some women are fat, and some are thin. . . . That's why there's both a full moon and a crescent.

(*Three men appear in the room to the left.* FUJIMA, TOYAMA, KANEKO.)

IWAKICHI

It'll be time soon. I've got to finish the rest of today's love letter.

KAYOKO

Hurry, won't you? I'll read a book while I wait.

(IWAKICHI *goes to the desk and finishes his letter.* KAYOKO *sits and begins to read.*)

(*In the room to the left.*)

FUJIMA

(*He carries a parcel wrapped in a purple square of cloth.*) I am Shunnosuke Fujima. Very pleased to meet you.

TOYAMA

How do you do? My name is Toyama. And this is Mr. Kaneko from the Ministry of Foreign Affairs. (*Introduces the men.*) Mr. Fujima.

KANEKO

How do you do?

FUJIMA

You and Mr. Kaneko seem to be old friends.

TOYAMA

Yes. He was at the same school, but ahead of me.

FUJIMA

Oh, really? . . . My pupils are about to put on a dance-play. (*Hands them leaflets.*) Please take these. . . . Mrs. Tsukioka said she would buy a hundred tickets.

TOYAMA

(*jealously*) Mrs. Tsukioka wouldn't do that unless she were sure of making a profit.

KANEKO

No, she's not like you. She's the kind who makes losses, never a profit.

FUJIMA

Yes, that's the kind of person she really is.

KANEKO

(*firmly*) I am perfectly well aware what kind of person she is.

FUJIMA

(*changing the subject*) The plot of the dance-play is charming, if I must say so myself.

TOYAMA

(*looking at his watch*) She's late, isn't she? Summoning people here like that. . . . It's bad taste to keep a man waiting in a dress shop.

KANEKO

In the reign of Louis XIV they used to receive men in their boudoirs. And when a man wanted to compliment a woman he'd say something like "Who does the shading under your eyes?" (*He says it in French.*)

FUJIMA

Excuse me? What was that?

(KANEKO *translates word for word.* TOYAMA *looks the other way.*)

FUJIMA

Shading under a woman's eyes is a lovely thing, isn't it? Like clouds hovering under the moon, you might say.

KANEKO

(*interested only in what he himself has to say*) That's the secret of all diplomacy. To ask who did the shading under a woman's eyes when you know perfectly well she did it herself.

TOYAMA

Mr. Kaneko is about to become an ambassador.

FUJIMA

(*bowing*) Congratulations.

(*In the room to the right.*)

IWAKICHI

I've written it. It's done. And very good this time.

KAYOKO

It must be a terrific strain always thinking up new things to say.

IWAKICHI

This is one of the more agreeable hardships of love.

KAYOKO

I'll leave it on my way home.

IWAKICHI

Sorry to bother you, Kayoko. Please don't lose it.

KAYOKO

You talk as if it wasn't just across the street. I couldn't lose it even if I wanted to. . . . Good night.

IWAKICHI

Good night, Kayoko.

KAYOKO

(*waving the letter as she stands in the door*) Maybe I will forget about the letter after all. I'm in a big hurry myself, you know.

IWAKICHI

You mustn't tease an old man like that.

(*In the room to the left.*)

KANEKO

She certainly is late.

TOYAMA

(*He stands in front of the mirror and fiddles with his necktie.*) Mrs. Tsukioka's taste in neckties always runs to something like this. I really hate loud ties.

FUJIMA

This is a tobacco-case Mrs. Tsukioka gave me when I succeeded as head of the company. The *netsuke* is more valuable than the case itself. Just have a look at it. (*He holds it up to the light.*) You'd never think it was made entirely of wood, would you? It's exactly like ivory, isn't it?

KANEKO

We civil servants must refuse all presents. There's always the suspicion of bribery. I envy artists.

FUJIMA

Everybody says that.

TOYAMA

(*in a tearful voice*) Damned old woman! Why should she have invited everybody except me?

KAYOKO

(*out of breath*) Oh, excuse me. Is the Madame here?

TOYAMA

She went to the shop a couple of minutes ago. I think she had some business to do.

KAYOKO

Now what am I going to do?

TOYAMA

Is it something urgent?

KAYOKO

Yes. It's a letter. I give one to Madame every day, at somebody's request. . . .

KANEKO

(*haughtily*) I'll take care of it.

KAYOKO

(*hesitantly*) It's very kind of you. . . .

KANEKO

I'll accept responsibility.

KAYOKO

I'm much obliged. Please. (*Exits.*)

TOYAMA

What a terrific hurry that girl is in!

KANEKO

(*He reads the address on the envelope.*) Well, I never! It says: "To the princess of the laurel of the moon."

FUJIMA

Very romantic, isn't it?

KANEKO

You didn't write it yourself, by any chance?

FUJIMA

You're joking. When a dancing-teacher has the time to write love letters, he holds hands instead.

KANEKO

The sender is one Iwakichi.

FUJIMA

He writes a very good hand, whoever he is.

TOYAMA

Just imagine—calling the Madame a "princess of the laurel of the moon"! I don't think I've ever seen a laurel. Is it a very big tree?

FUJIMA

Only around the middle, I think.

KANEKO

There's no accounting for tastes, is there? Let's see—there's a French expression something like that—

MADAME

(*Enters. She is unusually tall.*) It's so good to find you all here.

TOYAMA

A love letter's come for you.

MADAME

I wonder who it can be from. There are five or six gentlemen who might be sending me one.

KANEKO

Your affairs are touch-and-go, I take it?

MADAME

Yes, that's right. I never forget my defenses.

TOYAMA

Your armor must take a lot of material.

MADAME

Darling boy! You always say such amusing things.

FUJIMA

(*dramatically*) "The princess of the laurel of the moon," I presume?

MADAME

Oh, is *that* the love letter you're talking about? In that case, it's not for me.

KANEKO

Don't try to fool us.

MADAME

You're quite mistaken. It's for Mrs. Tsukioka.

ALL

What?

MADAME

(*sitting*) These letters are driving me simply frantic. They're from the janitor who works in the building across the street. An old man almost seventy. He's fallen in love with Mrs. Tsukioka, from having seen her through the window.

KANEKO

That doesn't surprise me. They say that the aged tend to be farsighted. (*He laughs, amused at his own joke.*) I can't wait to grow old. It must be very convenient being farsighted.

MADAME

The old man has sent her dozens—no, hundreds—of letters.

TOYAMA

If he sent out all his letters to different women, one of them might have been successful.

KANEKO

There's something in what you say. But if, after all, love were a question of probability, the probability for one woman might be the same as the probability for innumerable women.

FUJIMA

Have you shown her the letters? Mrs. Tsukioka, I mean.

MADAME

How could I possibly show them to her? I've used them all as comb-wipers.

TOYAMA

Do combs get as dirty as all that?

MADAME

They're for my dogs' combs. I have five wire-haired fox terriers. They shut their eyes in positive rapture when I comb them.

KANEKO

Which runs faster—love or a dog?

FUJIMA

Which gets dirty faster?

MADAME

It makes me quite giddy to talk with such enchanting men.

KANEKO

Sidetracked again. What's happened to the love letters?

MADAME

This is what has happened. The one who's been delivering the letters is that sweet girl from the office across the way.

TOYAMA

The girl who was just here? What's sweet about her?

MADAME

She's a well-behaved, good girl, and I've become so fond of her that I've been accepting the letters every day. But I've never dreamed of giving one to Mrs. Tsukioka.

KANEKO

If the girl knew that, she'd never give you another one.

MADAME

You'll have to excuse me. Just put yourself in my place. If Mrs. Tsukioka should read them and get upset—
(*Knock at the door.*)

MADAME

Now what shall I do? It's Mrs. Tsukioka.

KANEKO

Attention. (HANAKO *enters.*) Salute!

TOYAMA

(*clutching her*) It's cruel of you. To be late again.

FUJIMA

We were expecting you at any minute.

MADAME

You always look lovely, no matter how often I see you. (HANAKO *does not answer. She smilingly removes her gloves.*)

MADAME

(*trying to take the initiative*) Everybody's been waiting so impatiently I don't want to waste another minute. We'll start the fitting at once. (*She examines Hanako from the front and from behind.*) A dressy model really suits your naturally elegant line best, Mrs. Tsukioka. But in a spring suit, you know, I think we should try for a different effect. With your figure you can carry off something sporty. This time I've been really daring in the cut. The lines are simple, divinely simple. Just the barest of pleats on the sides of the waist, as you suggested. Very effective in bringing out the accents. . . . And now, would you mind stepping into the fitting-room? We can have a leisurely cup of coffee afterward.

KANEKO

A love letter came for you, Mrs. Tsukioka. Guess how old the man is who sent it. Twenty? Thirty? Older?
(HANAKO *holds up one finger.*)

TOYAMA

No, no. He's not a high-school student.
(HANAKO *with a smile holds up two fingers. The others shake their heads. She holds up one more finger each time until finally, with a look of incredulity on her face, she holds up seven.*)

KANEKO

You've guessed it, at last. A blushing seventy. I'm told he's the janitor in the building across the street.
(*The* MADAME, *flustered, lowers the blinds.* IWAKICHI, *in the room to the right, stares fixedly at the shut window. During the interval* KANEKO *hands the letter to* HANAKO. *She opens it. The others stand behind her and read over her shoulder.*)

TOYAMA

(*reads*) "Please read this thirtieth expression of my love, and take it to your heart," it says. Madame's been lying again. She said there were hundreds of letters. You know, Mrs. Tsukioka, the Madame has embezzled all the previous letters.

KANEKO

(*reads*) "My love grows only the stronger as the days go by. To heal the scars of the whip of love which torments my aged body from morn to night, I ask for one, for just one kiss." Isn't that touching? All he wants is one little kiss.

(*They all burst into laughter.*)

TOYAMA

Just one kiss? He's very modest in his demands.

FUJIMA

It really surprises me. The old men nowadays are younger at heart than we are.

MADAME

Is that the sort of thing he's been writing? I confess I haven't read any of his other efforts. (*The letter is passed to her.*) Oh, dear. (*reads*) "That which we call love is an eternal, unending sorrow." Trite, isn't it? He might just as well say: "That which we call vinegar, unlike honey, is an unending source of bitterness."

KANEKO

This old man thinks he's the only one who's suffering. Such conceit is detestable. All of us are suffering in exactly the same way. The only difference is that some people talk about it and others don't.

FUJIMA

That's because we have self-respect, isn't it?

TOYAMA

Even I can understand that much. I can't bear that tone which implies that he's the only one who knows real love, and the rest of us are all frivolous and fickle.

KANEKO

I'd be glad to show anyone who's willing to be shown how much repeated suffering we have to endure just in order to fool ourselves, all of us who are living in these depraved times.

FUJIMA

There's nothing you can do about people who are set in their ways. He must think there are special reserved seats for love.

TOYAMA

A romanticist.

MADAME

Little boys should not interfere in the conversation of grown-ups. The argument has become serious. (*She rings a bell.*) Isn't it enchanting, Mrs. Tsukioka, how heated men get over an argument?

KANEKO

(*as if he were delivering a speech*) I believe I may state without fear of contradiction that we are convinced that entities like this old man are abhorrent, and that such entities cannot further be tolerated by us—entities, that is, who believe in genuine feelings. There is not a village, no matter how remote, where the genuine and original Nagasaki sponge-cake is not sold. I despise any shopkeeper who would really believe such nonsense and fatuously sell the cake as the genuine article. It is far better to sell it knowing all along that it is fake. That makes the sale a cheat and a fraud, the splendid product of a conscious human mind. We have tongues to recognize the taste of the sponge-cake. Our loves begin from the tongue.

MADAME

How erotic!

KANEKO

The tongue admits the existence of no "genuine," of no "original." What it depends on is the sense of taste common to all men. The tongue can say: "This tastes good." Its natural modesty forbids it to say more. The "genuine and original" is merely a label people paste on the wrapping. The tongue confines itself to determining whether or not the sponge-cake tastes good.

SHOP ASSISTANT

(*Enters.*) Did you ring?

MADAME

It wasn't for sponge-cake. What was it? Oh yes, please bring five cups of coffee immediately.

ASSISTANT

Yes, Madame.

KANEKO

All questions are relative. Love is the architecture of the emotion of disbelief in genuine articles. That old man, on the other hand, is impure, polluted—he's making fools of us. He is delighted with himself, inflated with pride.

FUJIMA

I'm afraid what you say is much too difficult for someone like myself, who's never had an education, to follow, but I was told by my teacher that all disputes about who was the senior member of a company or which was the oldest tradition in a dance have nothing whatsoever to do with art. He said that the only true atmosphere for the dance is one where the gesture to the front and the gesture to the rear can be performed in absolute freedom. . . . That old man is so anxious to found a school for himself that he (*mimes dance action*) . . . one and two and over to the side . . . neglects the free, unconfined realms of the ecstasy of love.

TOYAMA

And what do you think about all this, Mrs. Tsukioka? It isn't very nice of you to keep so silent. But I suppose it isn't entirely distasteful to receive love letters even from such an old man. Isn't that the case? Say something, laurel of the moon.

MADAME

Mrs. Tsukioka had a refined upbringing, and I'm sure she dislikes arguments.

TOYAMA

But she's very fond of tormenting people all the same.

MADAME

That's a taste common to all beautiful women.

FUJIMA

And one which only becomes beautiful women, they say.

MADAME

When it comes to colors, the ones which suit her best are the difficult ones like green.

KANEKO

Those, of course, are the colors she doesn't wear in public. She saves them for her nightgowns, and pretends she doesn't know they become her.

TOYAMA

I can testify that Mrs. Tsukioka never wears green nightgowns.

KANEKO

You've become increasingly cheeky of late.

MADAME

Come, come.
(THE ASSISTANT *enters with the coffee. They all drink unhurriedly.*)

(*In the room to the right.*)

IWAKICHI

I wonder what's the matter. Why don't they open the curtains? Oh, the suspense. All I could get was just the barest glimpse of her. . . . And I was so sure that tonight she would take pity on me and at least stand at the window and smile at me, like a picture in a frame. . . . But I'm still not giving up hope. . . . No, I won't give up hope.

(*In the room to the left.*)

KANEKO

Well, now.

FUJIMA

Oops. (*He spills coffee on his lap and wipes it.*)

KANEKO

What is it?

FUJIMA

Just now as I was drinking my coffee, a fine idea came to me.

KANEKO

I have also been considering what we might do to teach that old man a little lesson. What do you say, Mrs. Tsukioka? In general . . .

FUJIMA

My plan was . . .

KANEKO

(*paying him no attention*) In general, such entities are incapable of seeing the light unless they have once been administered a sound thrashing. We need show him no pity simply because he's an old man. It is essential to make him realize that where he lives is a little room nobody will enter.

TOYAMA

You mean, human beings won't go in a dog's house?

KANEKO

(*recovering his good mood*) Yes, exactly.

FUJIMA

My plan is this. (*He unfolds the parcel wrapped in purple silk, revealing a small hand-drum.*) Do you see this?

MADAME

It's a drum, isn't it?

FUJIMA

It's a prop for my forthcoming dance-play. Oh, since I mentioned the play, I must thank you, Mrs. Tsukioka . . . the tickets. . . . At any rate, about the drum. Shall I beat it for you? (*He beats it.*) You see, it doesn't make the least sound. It looks exactly like a real drum, but instead of a skin, which is essential of course, it's covered with damask.

TOYAMA

You mean they've invented a drum that doesn't make any noise?

FUJIMA

No, as I was saying, it's a prop.

KANEKO

And what do you propose to do with it?

FUJIMA

To attach a note to this drum and throw it into the old man's room. I've had the most wonderful idea about what to write in the note.

MADAME

That sounds fascinating. Tell us.

FUJIMA

In the note we should write: "Please beat this drum." Do you follow me? "Please beat this drum. If the sound of your drum can be heard in this room above the street noises, I will grant your wish." That's all.

TOYAMA

Excellent idea! That will take the old man down a peg or two.

KANEKO

Don't you think you ought to add: "If the sound doesn't reach me, your wish will not be granted"?

FUJIMA

There's such a thing as an implied meaning.

KANEKO

In diplomatic correspondence you can't be too careful.

FUJIMA

(*excitedly*) Don't you think it's a good plan, Mrs. Tsukioka? I'll be glad to sacrifice this prop to protect you.

TOYAMA

For a customer who buys a hundred tickets, what's one drum?

FUJIMA

I'll thank you not to interpret it in that way. Mrs. Tsukioka, you do agree, don't you? (HANAKO *nods smilingly.*)

MADAME

It will be a great relief to me too. This will probably be the last day the old man will bother us.

FUJIMA

Let's have some paper and a pen.
(*They set about their preparations with animation.* FUJIMA *writes a note to attach to the drum. The* MADAME *draws the curtains.* HANAKO *is led to the window, which* KANEKO *opens.*)

KANEKO

His room is pitch dark. Are you sure the old man is there?

MADAME

The girl who comes as his messenger says that he stares at this window until Mrs. Tsukioka leaves.

KANEKO

Still, I wonder if our voices will reach him.

TOYAMA

That'll be my responsibility. Oh, doesn't it look pretty up here to see the neon lights everywhere?

FUJIMA

Who will throw the drum?

KANEKO

I will. I was quite a renowned pitcher in my high-school days. (*He limbers his arm by way of preparation.*)

TOYAMA

Hey! Iwakichi! Open your window!
(*The window opens.* IWAKICHI *timidly shows himself.*)

TOYAMA

Can you hear me? We're going to throw you something. Be sure to catch it.
(IWAKICHI *nods.* KANEKO *throws the drum.* IWAKICHI *barely gets it. He takes the drum to the desk.*)

IWAKICHI

What can this mean? She's sent me a drum. She's standing at the window looking at me. It's strange, when she looks straight this way it's all I can do to keep from hiding myself. I wonder if she's always hidden herself from me because I stared too much. . . . Oh, there's a note attached. (*reads*) At last my wish will be granted! What carries better than the sound of a drum, even above the traffic noise? It must be her elegant way of saying things —she can't pronounce a simple yes, but has to say it in some roundabout manner. . . . Oh, my heart hurts. It's never known such joy before. It's weak, like the stomach of a poor man's child before a feast. It hurts because it's been struck by happiness. . . . They're all waiting in the window over there. It must be for the fun of it. They think it will be amusing to hear an old man play the drum for the first time. . . . Ah, I've a good idea. I'll hang the drum on my laurel tree and beat it there. (*He kneels before the tree.*) Laurel, lovely, dear laurel, forgive me. I'm going to hang the drum in your green hair. Heavy, is it? Just be patient for a while. It becomes you. It becomes you very well, like a big beautiful ornament that has fallen from heaven into your hair. . . . It's all right, isn't it? Even when I begin to beat the drum, I won't shake your leaves. I've never before been so happy before you. Whenever I've seen you I've thought: My unhappiness has made you more beautiful, has made you put forth your leaves more abundantly. And it's true, my laurel, it's true.

TOYAMA

Hurry up and beat the drum. We're standing in the cold waiting for you.

IWAKICHI

All right! I'm going to beat it now, so listen! (*He strikes the drum. It makes no sound. He strikes the other side. It is also silent. He strikes frantically but to no avail.*) It doesn't make a noise. They've given me a drum that doesn't make a noise! I've been made a fool of. I've been played with. (*He sinks to the floor and weeps.*) What shall I do? What shall I do? A refined lady like that—to play such a low trick on me. It's something that should never have happened. It couldn't have happened.
(*The people at the window to the left laugh. The window is slammed shut.*)

Laugh! Go ahead and laugh! Laugh all you like! . . . You'll still be laughing when you die. You'll be laughing when you rot away. That won't happen to me. People who are laughed at don't die just like that. . . . People who are laughed at don't rot away. (*He opens the window at the back. Climbs out on the windowsill. He sits there motionlessly for a minute, sadly staring below. Then he pushes himself over the edge in a crumbling gesture. Shouts from below. Inarticulate cries from the crowd continue awhile.*)

(*In the room to the left they are all chatting and laughing. They cannot see the window from which the old man committed suicide, and they are unaware what has happened. Suddenly the door opens.*)

ASSISTANT

The janitor from the building across the way has just jumped out of the window and killed himself.

(They get up with confused outcries. Some rush to the window, others run toward the stairs. HANAKO *stands alone rigidly in the center of the stage.)*

(Late at night. The sky between the two buildings is now full of stars. A clock on a shelf in the room to the left gives forth two delicate chimes. The room is pitch dark. Presently there is a scratching sound of a key in the door. The door opens. A flashlight beam shines in. HANAKO *enters. She wears a half-length coat thrown over the shoulders of her evening gown. In one hand she holds a key, in the other a flashlight. She puts the key in her handbag. She goes to the window, opens it, and stares motionlessly at the window on the right.)*

HANAKO

(Her voice is low. She talks as if to someone present.) I've come. You told me to come and I've come. I slipped out of a party, even though it was the middle of the night. . . . Answer me, please. Aren't you there?

(The window at the back of the room to the right opens. The ghost of IWAKICHI *climbs in the window from which he jumped. He walks to the left. The window facing left gradually opens as he approaches it.)*

HANAKO

You've come. . . . You've really come.

IWAKICHI

I've been going back and forth between your dreams and this room.

HANAKO

You summoned me and I am here. But you still do not know me. You don't know how I was able to come.

IWAKICHI

Because I drew you here.

HANAKO

No. Without human strength no door opens for human beings to pass through.

IWAKICHI

Do you intend to deceive even a ghost?

HANAKO

Where would I get the strength? My strength was enough only to kill a pitiful old man. And even in that all I did was to nod. I did nothing else. (IWAKICHI *does not answer.*) Can you hear me? (IWAKICHI *nods.*) My voice carries even when I speak as low as this. But when I talk to people they can't hear me unless I shout. . . . It would have been better if voices had not carried between this room and yours.

IWAKICHI

The sky is full of stars. You can't see the moon. The moon has become covered with mud and fallen to earth. I was following the moon when I jumped. You might say that the moon and I committed suicide together.

HANAKO

(*looking down at the street*) Can you see the corpse of the moon anywhere? I can't. Only the all-night taxis cruising in the streets. There's a policeman walking there. He's stopped. But I don't think that means he's found a corpse. The policeman won't meet anything except the policeman who comes from the opposite direction. Is he a mirror, I wonder?

IWAKICHI

Do you think that ghosts meet only ghosts, and the moon meets only the moon?

HANAKO

In the middle of the night that's true of everything. (*She lights a cigarette.*)

IWAKICHI

I'm not a phantom any more. While I was alive I was a phantom. Now all that remains is what I used to dream about. Nobody can disappoint me any more.

HANAKO

From what I can see, however, you still aren't precisely the incarnation of love. I don't mean to criticize your growth of beard or your janitor's uniform or your sweaty undershirt— There's something lacking, something your love needs before it can assume a form. There's insufficient proof that your love in this world was real, if that was the only reason why you died.

IWAKICHI

Do you want proof from a ghost? (*He empties his pockets.*) Ghosts don't own anything. I've lost every possession which might have served as proof.

HANAKO

I am teeming with proofs. A woman simply crawls with proofs of love. When she has produced the last one, she is full of proofs that the love is gone. It's because women have the proofs that men can make love empty-handed.

IWAKICHI

Please don't show me such things.

HANAKO

A little while ago I opened the door and came in, didn't I? Where do you suppose I got the key to the door?

IWAKICHI

Please don't ask me such things.

HANAKO

I stole the key from Madame's pocket. My fingers are very nimble, you know. It gave me great pleasure to discover my skill at pickpocketing has still not left me.

IWAKICHI

I understand now. You're afraid of my tenacity, and you're trying to make me hate you. That must be it.

HANAKO

Then shall I show you? You gave me a very appropriate name, princess of the moon. I used otherwise to be known by the nickname of Crescent, from a tattoo on my belly. The tattoo of a crescent.

IWAKICHI

Ah-h-h.

HANAKO

It wasn't that I asked to have it tattooed myself. A man did it, violently. When I drink the crescent turns a bright red, but usually it is pale as a dead man's face.

IWAKICHI

Whore! You've made a fool of me twice. Once wasn't enough.

HANAKO

Once wasn't enough. Yes, that's right, it wasn't. For our love to be fulfilled, or for it to be destroyed.

IWAKICHI

You were poisoned by men who were untrue.

HANAKO

That's not so. Men who were untrue molded me.

IWAKICHI

I was made a fool of because I was true.

HANAKO

That's not so. You were made a fool of because you were old.

(*The room to the right becomes red with the wrath of the ghost. The laurel tree on which the drum had been hung appears in the glow.*)

IWAKICHI

Don't you feel ashamed of yourself? I'll place a curse on you.

HANAKO

That doesn't frighten me in the least. I'm strong now. It's because I've been loved.

IWAKICHI

By whom?

HANAKO

By you.

IWAKICHI

Was it the strength of my love that made you tell the truth?

HANAKO

Look at me. It's not the real me you love. (*She laughs.*) You tried to place a curse on me. Clumsy men are all like that.

IWAKICHI

No, no. I am in love with you, passionately. Everybody in the world of the dead knows it.

HANAKO

Nobody knows it in this world.

IWAKICHI

Because the drum didn't sound?

HANAKO

Yes, because I couldn't hear it.

IWAKICHI

It was the fault of the drum. A damask drum makes no noise.

HANAKO

It wasn't the fault of the drum that it didn't sound.

IWAKICHI

I yearn for you, even now.

HANAKO

Even now! You've been dead all of a week.

IWAKICHI

I yearn for you. I shall try to make the drum sound.

HANAKO

Make it sound. I have come to hear it.

IWAKICHI

I will. My love will make a damask drum thunder. (*The ghost of* IWAKICHI *strikes the drum. It gives forth a full sound.*) It sounded! It sounded! You heard it, didn't you?

HANAKO

(*smiling slyly*) I can't hear a thing.

IWAKICHI

You can't hear this? It's not possible. Look. I'll strike it once for every letter I wrote you. Once, twice, you can hear it, I know, three, four, the drum has sounded. (*The drum sounds.*)

HANAKO

I can't hear it. Where is a drum sounding?

IWAKICHI

You can't hear it? You're lying. You can't hear this? Ten, eleven. You can't hear this?

HANAKO

I can't. I can't hear any drum.

IWAKICHI

It's a lie! (*in a fury*) I won't let you say it—that you can't hear what I can. Twenty, twenty-one. It's sounded.

HANAKO

I can't hear it. I can't hear it.

IWAKICHI

Thirty, thirty-one, thirty-two. . . . You can't say you don't hear it. The drum is beating. A drum that never should have sounded is sounding.

HANAKO

Ah, hurry and sound it. My ears are longing to hear the drum.

IWAKICHI

Sixty-six, sixty-seven. . . . Could it possibly be that only my ears can hear the drum?

HANAKO

(*in despair, to herself*) Ah, he's just the same as living men.

IWAKICHI

(*in despair, to himself*) Who can prove it—that she hears the drum?

HANAKO

I can't hear it. I still can't hear it.

IWAKICHI

(*weakly*) Eighty-nine, ninety, ninety-one. . . . It will soon be over. Have I only imagined I heard the sound of the drum? (*The drum goes on sounding.*) It's useless. A waste of time. The drum won't sound at all, will it? Beat it and beat it as I may, it's a damask drum.

HANAKO

Hurry, strike it so I can hear. Don't give up. Hurry, so it strikes my ears. (*She stretches her hand from the window.*) Don't give up!

IWAKICHI

Ninety-four, ninety-five. . . . Completely useless. The drum doesn't make a sound. What's the use of beating a drum that is silent? . . . Ninety-six, ninety-seven. . . . Farewell, my laurel princess, farewell. . . . Ninety-eight, ninety-nine. . . . Farewell, I've ended the hundred strokes. . . . Farewell.

(*The ghost disappears. The beating stops.* HANAKO *stands alone, an empty look on her face.* TOYAMA *rushes in excitedly.*)

TOYAMA

Is that where you've been? Oh, I'm so relieved. . . . We've all been out searching for you. What happened to you? Running off like that in the middle of the night. What happened to you? (*He shakes her.*) Get a hold on yourself.

HANAKO

(*as in a dream*) I would have heard if he had only struck it once more.

CURTAIN

KANTAN

CHARACTERS:

JIRŌ

KIKU

(Dream Personages):

THE BEAUTY

DANCERS

GENTLEMEN

PRIVATE SECRETARY

CELEBRATED PHYSICIAN

DOCTORS

FEMALE EMPLOYEE

(*Before the curtain.*)

KIKU

(*Her voice is heard from offstage.*) It's so wonderful you've come.

JIRŌ

(*also offstage*) It's been ten years, hasn't it, Kiku?

KIKU

You've grown so big. . . . Oh, I'll carry it.

JIRŌ

No, I've got it. That's all right.

KIKU

Please let me have it. I can manage. It's only a suitcase. (KIKU *enters with the suitcase. She is a woman of about forty. She is followed by* JIRŌ, *a young man of eighteen, in a double-breasted suit.*)

JIRŌ

(*looking around him*) It's still pitch dark.

KIKU

It'll be light soon. The days are long at this time of year. Please come in. (*She kneels and puts her hand on the curtain. It opens before* KIKU *and* JIRŌ, *who have their backs to the audience. In the center, to the rear, is a shōji, a Japanese double-paneled paper door. An enormous number of birds, flowers, and other paper cut-outs are suspended from the ceiling.*)

JIRŌ

Oh, that's pretty! It's fixed up exactly the way my room used to be when I was a boy, isn't it?

KIKU

Yes, it is. I don't want ever to forget that room. It was where I brought you up. This room is modeled on the one in your house in Tokyo. I wanted it always to stay the same.

JIRŌ

The house with that room burned down.

KIKU

I know, but nothing has changed here.

JIRŌ

(*flicking the paper decorations hanging from the ceiling and making them spin*) It feels just as if I've come back to that house—the one that burned down. How long has it been since you fixed up the room this way?

KIKU

Ten years—ever since I left your family's service. I put up new paper ornaments once a month.

JIRŌ

It's unbelievable how women cling to the past. It never ceases to amaze me.

KIKU

Be as disagreeable as you like! When you were five you were already talking like that.

JIRŌ

(*getting down on the floor*) Building blocks! This must be the set my parents gave you as a remembrance of me. My old building blocks—how many years has it been since I played with them? Yes, this little car goes through under the arch.

KIKU

The arch is a trifle too low. You always used to lift it to let the automobile pass under.

JIRŌ

The car had an accident.

KIKU

Excuse me?

JIRŌ

The real car, I mean.

KIKU

Where was the accident?

JIRŌ

I came on the eight o'clock bus yesterday evening, the last one, and just about halfway here it broke down, at the pass.

KIKU

Accidents are always happening there.

JIRŌ

We waited and waited, but nobody came to fix it. I put my coat over my head and had a little nap inside the bus. It was after three when I woke. I walked the last couple of miles.

KIKU

All alone at night on the road?

JIRŌ

You couldn't get lost on that road. Besides, it was light. The stars were shining.

KIKU

(*going to sit in another place*) You know, premonitions really do come true. I suddenly woke up in the middle of the night and got dressed. I felt so restless I knew I'd never get to sleep again.

JIRŌ

Did you think I was coming?

KIKU

Why, yes. I knew I would see you again some day.

JIRŌ

Did you imagine I'd journey all the way here just for a visit?

KIKU

Nobody would come to such a place to make money. . . . But even if it's for money, I'm happy, very happy all the same, just to have been able to see you.

JIRŌ

I can imagine. It's a proof, I suppose, that everything's at an end for me. I'd never have decided otherwise to make my way to such a place. My life is finished.

KIKU

What a strange thing to say! You're just eighteen! How can life be over at eighteen? Aren't you exaggerating a little?

JIRŌ

I may be only eighteen, but I've got enough sense to know when my own life is finished.

KIKU

Your head's not getting bald! Your back's not bent! You haven't a wrinkle on your face!

JIRŌ

You can't see them, that's all. My hair may *look* black, but it's really snow-white; my teeth are gone, and my back is bent double.

KIKU

I don't seem to understand.

JIRŌ

No, you wouldn't.
(*Pause.*)

KIKU

Young master . . . have you . . . I mean . . . a young lady somewhere, perhaps?

JIRŌ

Are you asking if I'm in love?

KIKU

Yes, has that happened to you?

JIRŌ

(*brusquely*) I've never loved and I've never been loved by anyone.

KIKU

Then it's not disappointed love, is it?

JIRŌ

Don't be silly, Kiku. Disappointed love? That's for children.

KIKU

(*widening her eyes*) Oh? Then what can it be? You haven't been betrayed by a friend?

JIRŌ

A friend? I've never had a friend.

KIKU

Possibly you've failed your examinations?

JIRŌ

I gave up school long ago.

KIKU

Then I suppose you must have been badly treated by the world.

JIRŌ

I've spent my time loafing at home.

KIKU

Then why should your life be at an end? Why, before it has even begun?

JIRŌ

It was over before it began.

KIKU

It makes me afraid when you tease and poke fun at me that way.

JIRŌ

Silly old woman— Don't flatter yourself.

KIKU

I know what it is. You hadn't enough sleep last night and you're all on edge. Why don't you lie down for a while? Have a good rest while Kiku prepares your breakfast. Then you'll feel refreshed. I'll lay out the bedding.

JIRŌ

(*Stands, opens the* shōji *a little, and peers outside.*) Kiku, why do all the plants and bushes in the garden droop their heads? There's not a flower blooming. It's weird, that garden—pitch black and absolutely still.

KIKU

(*taking out the bedding*) The garden is dead. The flowers don't bloom, so there isn't any fruit either. It's been like this for a long time.

JIRŌ

Do you mean by "a long time" ever since your husband left you?

KIKU

You know all about it, then.

JIRŌ

I didn't learn that from a book. The other day on the Ginza I met a sandwichman dressed up to look like Chaplin. He's a bachelor, and his only pleasures in life are to drink coffee and go to the movies. Between the coffee and the movies he has all he needs to keep happy. He told me about it.

KIKU

What did he tell you?

JIRŌ

About the pillow, of course.

KIKU

(*falling back in consternation*) Ah-h——!

JIRŌ

He said you have a very peculiar pillow here. Now stop—don't look so terrified. All I'm telling you is what this Chaplin told me.

KIKU

You mustn't take such stories seriously.

JIRŌ

Have it your own way. At any rate, you have a strange pillow. I don't know how you got it, but what counts is that it's here. . . . Once your husband happened to find the pillow—it was in the summer, I'm told—and he took a nap on it. You were doing some shopping in town at the time. That night when you returned your husband wasn't there any more. Where could he have gone? He's never come back since.

KIKU

Please—enough. Enough, I beg you. It's too painful for me to talk about these things.

JIRŌ

Ever since that day the lilies and the carnations and all the other flowers in your garden have stopped blooming. That's true, isn't it?

KIKU

Yes, it certainly is. . . . The pillow came originally—a long time ago—from a place in China called Kantan. It was passed down from one generation to another until it finally became an heirloom of my family.

JIRŌ

But why is it when you sleep on that pillow . . .

KIKU

I don't know why it is. I've always been too afraid to sleep on it myself.

JIRŌ

You know what Chaplin told me? He said if you sleep on that pillow and dream for a while, it makes the whole world seem meaningless afterward. Then, when you look at your wife's face, you can't imagine why you've been living with such a woman. He said that he himself ran away from home immediately.

KIKU

(*Weeps.*)

JIRŌ

I'm sorry, Kiku. Did I make you cry? I'm sorry.

KIKU

Don't apologize, young master. It's not in the least your fault. . . .

JIRŌ

But Kiku, haven't you even once used the pillow since then?

KIKU

Shall I tell you everything? I've used it three times.

JIRŌ

Three times?

KIKU

Yes. After my husband left me that way—some men have very odd tastes in women, you know, and quite a few advances were made to me. . . . Each time that pillow came in handy.

JIRŌ

Came in handy? You mean the men all ran away?

KIKU

Yes, that is . . . It's very hard to explain.

JIRŌ

Say it, please say it!

KIKU

It's hard to tell, but it's nothing I'm ashamed of.

JIRŌ

Say it, Kiku, please come out with it. (*He touches her knee.*)

KIKU

I remember how when you begged me for cakes you used to shake my knee that way.

JIRŌ

Tell me! Don't change the subject.

KIKU

Very well, I'll tell you. I was able, thanks to the pillow, to preserve my chastity.

JIRŌ

What do you mean by that?

KIKU

You see, when things got difficult I would offer the man the pillow. It didn't matter what sort of man he was when he went to sleep—when he opened his eyes the whole world seemed preposterous to him, and he wouldn't so much as glance at me. Then, young master, one by one they would set off on their wanderings, never to be seen again.

JIRŌ

What exactly do you mean when you say that the world seemed preposterous to them?

KIKU

Women, money, fame—

JIRŌ

In that case, nothing's going to surprise me. Woman's a soap-bubble, money's a soap-bubble, fame's another, and the world we live in is only what we see reflected in these soap-bubbles. That much I know.

KIKU

Only in words.

JIRŌ

No, that's not true. I've seen through all of them. That's why my life is finished. And that's why, Kiku, I'm the only man who can sleep on that pillow in perfect safety.

KIKU

I wonder. It makes me sad to think that after you sleep on the pillow you may look at Kiku as if she was a stranger, and then vanish and never come back.

JIRŌ

Don't worry. I'm absolutely safe. I'll never become like that Chaplin.

KIKU

Chaplin?

JIRŌ

Yes—I mean—your husband.

KIKU

How do you know?

JIRŌ

Look, I know everything.
(*Pause.*)

KIKU

Then shall we make an agreement, young master? If the pillow makes you wander off somewhere, will you take me with you?

JIRŌ

But I tell you, it's all settled. The pillow won't have any effect on me. It was for the express purpose of proving that it wouldn't change me that I came here.

KIKU

All the same, when I look at your face, I feel as though I were looking at water flowing far away.

JIRŌ

What are you talking about? It'll be morning soon. Hurry up and bring the pillow.

KIKU

If you would only please promise to take me along . . .

JIRŌ

Even if I did, it wouldn't do any good. I'm not leaving.

KIKU

But just supposing, one chance in a million . . .

JIRŌ

You're counting on that one chance in a million, aren't you? You want to go look for your husband.

KIKU

(*in confusion*) I'd never do such a silly—

JIRŌ

Yes, yes, you would! You're blushing!

KIKU

You don't understand, young master. It's a very painful thing to wait.

JIRŌ

How would it be if for once you slept on the pillow? Then you could forget all about your husband.

KIKU

I'm too afraid. I'm frightened what the pillow might do.

JIRŌ

If you're afraid, then don't. Hurry up with the pillow!

KIKU

I had been thinking I would just molder away here in peace, but, young master, because of you my wretched hopes . . .

JIRŌ

It's one chance in a million, Kiku, that's all.

KIKU

Very well. I'll bring the pillow.

JIRŌ

Oh, I'm sleepy, horribly sleepy. Hurry up. It'll soon be morning.

KIKU

Yes, in a moment. (*She goes out.*)

CHORUS

The pillow is blameless
The pillowed head is to blame
Little birds have ceased to sing
Flowers bloom no more
But the pillow is blameless
And man is to blame
The pillow is blameless
Little birds are to blame
The pillow is blameless
Flowers are to blame
Day in, day out, the woods are green
But rustle in the wind, so uselessly

They flutter, they flutter. . . .
The unblossoming lily is to blame.

(*While this is being sung* JIRŌ *removes his coat and lies on the bed.* KIKU *enters with the pillow, which she places under* JIRŌ's *head. She leaves. From the center rear, as the chorus ends, the* BEAUTY *enters. She wears a mask and is dressed in an evening dress.*)

BEAUTY

Jirō . . . Jirō . . .

CHORUS

Wake up . . . wake up . . .

BEAUTY

Jirō . . . Jirō . . .

CHORUS

Wake up . . . wake up . . .

JIRŌ

(*waking and sitting up in bed*) What is it? Who are you? (*in admiration*) Well—you're quite a beauty!

BEAUTY

Guess who I am.

JIRŌ

That's what I dislike most about women. They never tell you their names without making a fuss.

BEAUTY

You like straightforward women, do you? How old-fashioned! Unless a woman puts up a little resistance she's not very interesting, you know.

JIRŌ

Don't bother me with your trite phrases.

BEAUTY

That's my name: Trite.

JIRŌ

I've never heard such a stupid name.

BEAUTY

But you see, if Trite becomes a proper name, then Trite phrases are no longer trite phrases.

JIRŌ

They shouldn't become puns like that either.

BEAUTY

Oh, your hands are trembling like butterflies! I'll catch them for you. (*She takes his hands inside her own.*) I've caught them! If I hadn't done that, your hands would have flown away.

JIRŌ

You've got a wild imagination.

BEAUTY

(*smiling archly*) I'm only imitating you.

JIRŌ

What do you think happens when a woman who knows men imitates a man who doesn't know women?

BEAUTY

What complicated things you ask, little man.

JIRŌ

You wind up with a woman who doesn't know men.

BEAUTY

If you're going to say things like that and look so pleased with yourself . . . Let's drink the liquor Trite has brought for you.

JIRŌ

Not for me. I don't like getting drunk.

BEAUTY

There's no liquor that doesn't make you drunk.

JIRŌ

That's why I don't like liquor.

BEAUTY

You say that now, but in ten years you'll be a real drunkard.

JIRŌ

I dare say. But why must I drink now just because I'm going to become a drunkard in ten years?

BEAUTY

What adorable eyes you have when you argue. Eyes that get drunk on your own arguments.

JIRŌ

Oh— Something frightening just flashed in your eyes.

BEAUTY

What was it?

JIRŌ

Sometimes a wolf goes through a woman's eyes.

BEAUTY

It's usually an error on the part of the shepherd.

JIRŌ

I don't like you in the least.

BEAUTY

All the same, we'll be married in six months.

JIRŌ

I'm not in love with you in the least.

BEAUTY

Whether you love me or you don't, it won't be long before we're married.

JIRŌ

Nobody likes the dust that gathers inside trouser pockets, but it gathers all the same, and goes on gathering for a lifetime. Laundries are not very obliging.

BEAUTY

(*in a singsong intonation*) Laundries are not very obliging. . . . Then we'll go on our honeymoon.

JIRŌ

Endless tips, and scenery viewed to the accompaniment of yawns; badly taken souvenir photos, and a circus like the kind you see as a child at a county fair—the monkey who walks a tightrope with a parasol . . .

BEAUTY

You talk as if you've already experienced it.

JIRŌ

All a honeymoon is, is a test of one's equipment, isn't it?

BEAUTY

(*clapping her hands*) What enchanting things you say, even if you *are* a child.

JIRŌ

After the first five years you'll look shiny as a well-ridden bicycle. And that will be that. From then on the bicycle will only get rustier and rustier. What people mean by a good husband is someone who never makes his wife feel that he could walk, even if he hadn't a bicycle.

BEAUTY

You think you'll finish me off with such words, but that's where you're mistaken. Your adversary has not been so much as scratched! Think. In the morning I'll get up ahead of you and make the toast and boil an egg. You'll stand the egg on end and crack the shell with the edge of your spoon so— Tap-tap-tap—

JIRŌ

What's all that? An egg's an egg.

BEAUTY

Then I'll say: "How clumsy you are. Let me do it!"

JIRŌ

You will! I hate people who interfere.

BEAUTY

"Oh dear, this egg is boiled hard!"

JIRŌ

Women's cooking is always like that. Things they cook are either boiled too long or served raw, they're too salty or too sweet.

BEAUTY

See how nicely I've peeled your egg for you. Now I'm going to put it in your mouth (*suddenly kissing him*).

JIRŌ

I can't breathe! It's painful.

BEAUTY

What a silly one you are. You don't understand anything at all. What do you think you have nostrils for? It's so you can breathe with your nose while you're kissing.

JIRŌ

I hate breathing through my nose.

BEAUTY

No wonder your mouth is always wide open.

JIRŌ

You're pretty, you know.

BEAUTY

At last, you've opened your eyes.

JIRŌ

I felt as if a mask kissed me.

BEAUTY

That's what women's kisses are like.

JIRŌ

You really are pretty. But if you strip away the skin, what have you got but a skull?

BEAUTY

You're horrid. I've never thought about such a thing. (*She touches her face.*)

JIRŌ

Do you suppose that some skulls rank as beauties among their kind?

BEAUTY

I imagine so. Some must, I'm sure.

JIRŌ

What extraordinary confidence! But when I was kissed just now I knew that underneath your cheeks your bones were laughing.

BEAUTY

If my face laughs the bones laugh too.

JIRŌ

Is that what you have to say for yourself? You should say when your face laughs your bones are laughing. That's for sure. But the bones of your face laugh also when your face is crying. The bones say: "Laugh if you want. Cry if you want. Our turn will be coming soon."

BEAUTY

The bones' turn! How divine to think of such a thing.

JIRŌ

Women have only two terms of criticism: "How divine!" and "Silly!" Those are the only two.

BEAUTY

What an adorable little cynic you are!
(*She looks fondly at* JIRŌ. *Suddenly, from a cradle at stage-right an infant's squalling is heard.*)

BEAUTY

Our baby has been born!

JIRŌ

Humph. It's like toast popping from the toaster.

BEAUTY

(*peeping into the cradle*) Isn't he sweet? Does baby know Mama? Peek-a-boo! I see you!

JIRŌ

Cut it out, won't you? It's stupid. You're not a department-store Santa Claus.

BEAUTY

Shall we go see Papa? Shall we? You mustn't cry now. Papa's still a child himself, but he's very difficult about some things. (*bringing the cradle beside* JIRŌ's *bed*) Papa! Look, papa! It's our first child!

JIRŌ

Well, well. Our first skull?

BEAUTY

What do you think? Does he look like you or like me?

JIRŌ

(*turning away*) A baby is born. Into this dark, gloomy world. His mother's womb was more cheerful. Why should he ever have wanted to leave it for a gloomier place? Little idiot. I can't understand him at all.

BEAUTY

He's winking! He's laughed.

JIRŌ

The bones have already learned to laugh. Don't you think it's frightening? Don't you?

BEAUTY

Peek-a-boo!

JIRŌ

I hope and pray this is only a dream.

BEAUTY

Peek-a-boo! I see you!

JIRŌ

Only a dream . . .

BEAUTY

He's looking at Papa and smiling.

JIRŌ

Is he? Do you think he looks like me or like you?

BEAUTY

You may say what you will, but I know deep at heart you're interested in him.

JIRŌ

Huh? Which of us does he look like?

BEAUTY

If you make such a frightening face he'll start crying. Now that you ask, I regret to say he looks more like his father than he does me.

JIRŌ

Does he?

BEAUTY

The eyebrows, the nose, the mouth . . . I can see your face faintly traced behind his.

JIRŌ

Then he looks like me.

BEAUTY

It should make you happier.

JIRŌ

I don't like it, for him to look like me.

BEAUTY

You're so modest.

JIRŌ

How disgusting, a brat who resembles me has been born.

BEAUTY

(*wailing*) Stop it!

JIRŌ

(*picking up an ash tray from his bedside and furiously banging the inside of the cradle with it*) I'll show him!

BEAUTY

Stop it! What are you doing? Stop it!

JIRŌ

He's dead.

BEAUTY

My little son! How dreadful! How dreadful!

JIRŌ

He's better off this way. If he had lived to grow up he would sooner or later have suffered because of his resemblance to his father. That's the experience everybody goes through.

BEAUTY

You horrible man! You're jealous even of your own child.

JIRŌ

That's right. I won't allow anybody to look like me.

BEAUTY

(*weeping*) Monster . . . dreadful monster . . .

JIRŌ

Look, the bones are laughing.

BEAUTY

I suppose I love you all the same.

JIRŌ

I should hope so.

BEAUTY

Now I understand! You killed the baby because you love me. You were afraid that someone might come between us. That was it, wasn't it? I love you. I love you so much. At last I understand! You're a very passionate man. I didn't realize how passionate you are. It was silly of me. The baby is already a thing of the past—I forgive you. I forgive you everything, every last thing.

JIRŌ

I wonder how a woman's self-conceit can be so conveniently arranged?

BEAUTY

Jirō, in exchange, don't leave me.

JIRŌ

If you will be a faithful wife to me.

BEAUTY

I will! I'll do anything. I'll scrub the floors, sweep, mend your clothes, anything. If you tell me to walk naked through the streets, I'll do that too.

JIRŌ

A splendid resolution. First of all, you must never be jealous.

BEAUTY

Yes. I'll put up with anything, anything.

JIRŌ

(*stretching*) Let me see. Oh, yes. I am a father who's lost his child. I need some sort of consolation. Something to cheer me up. A distraction, like other men have.

BEAUTY

That's right, enjoy yourself all you like. I'll just watch. No matter what you do, I'll just watch and never once get jealous. I'll be patient and watch. Just to be able to look at you will be all the satisfaction I ask for. I'm happy. (*A strange, sensuous music is heard.*) I shall be silent and look at you, like a lily.

JIRŌ

What a lily! Well, you can look at me all you like. It doesn't cost anything to look.

(*The* BEAUTY *sits in a child's chair to stage-right. Three half-naked* DANCING GIRLS *enter. They wear masks. They form a circle and dance.*)

CHORUS

The pillow is blameless
If you dance the sun shines, the clouds grow
  bright
If you dance your life is not the same
The dance is blameless
If you dance your shadow is not the same.

FIRST DANCER

Jirō . . . Jirō . . .

CHORUS

Dance! Dance! Dance!

SECOND DANCER

Jirō . . . Jirō . . .

CHORUS

Dance! Dance! Dance!

THIRD DANCER

Jirō . . . Jirō . . .

CHORUS

Dance! Dance! Dance!
(*The three* DANCERS *unsuccessfully attempt to draw* JIRŌ *into the dance. He remains obdurate. He lies in bed, his head propped on his elbows, watching them. The* DANCERS *finally give up and sit on the bed around him.*)

FIRST DANCER

What beautiful eyes! I've never seen a man with such divine eyes.

JIRŌ

You say that because you see your own face reflected in them. Isn't that it?

FIRST DANCER

That's not a very nice answer.

SECOND DANCER

What beautiful teeth you have!

JIRŌ

I brush them every morning in sulphuric acid.

SECOND DANCER

Oh, how ferocious! Isn't he wonderful!

JIRŌ

You have a nice fat hand. It looks good enough to eat.

SECOND DANCER

Eat all you like. Another one will grow back.

DANCERS

(*Laugh.*)

JIRŌ

Can't you say anything without laughing? There's nothing more boring than when a woman starts to laugh. You never know how long it's going to last.

DANCERS

Doesn't he say the most amusing things?

THIRD DANCER

It's my turn now. I love Jirō's forehead. It's white and broad, like an airplane runway.

JIRŌ

It'd be a pity to leave it as a runway. One of you ought to cultivate it and grow something there.

FIRST DANCER

I'll do it. . . .

SECOND DANCER

No, I will.

THIRD DANCER

Let me!

FIRST DANCER

Let's *all* cultivate it.

JIRŌ

All right, all right . . . Just supposing you cultivate it. You plant seeds—carrots and turnips, say. Before you know it, the carrots grow. The turnips grow. You pull the carrots and turnips from my forehead. You boil them to a pulp. Then you pile them on a plate. . . .

FIRST DANCER

Yes, and then?

JIRŌ

You eat them up.

FIRST DANCER

Oh-h.

JIRŌ

You polish them off completely.

SECOND DANCER

And then?

THIRD DANCER

What a wonderful story! What happens next?

JIRŌ

That's all there is to it. That's what life is like. You get it, don't you? If you do, go away, and quickly.

FIRST DANCER

No, Jirō. I don't want to go.

JIRŌ

What a nuisance! Get out of here, quick!

SECOND DANCER

How rude he is! But I must say, there's something charming about his coldness.

JIRŌ

I said you're all nuisances. Go! Leave me!

THIRD DANCER

We'll do as you say, then, but give us a big tip, won't you?

FIRST DANCER

Next time we must spend a lot longer together.

SECOND DANCER

Jirō, I could tell you were generous from the first moment I laid eyes on you. I adore people with open faces.
(*While she is speaking there appears to stage-right a figure in a business suit. The* SECRETARY. *He wears the mask of a middle-aged gentleman. He makes a sign to the dancers and writes a check which he hands them. The* DANCERS *and the* BEAUTY *leave to the right.*)

JIRŌ

Who are you? Did you pay them? Sorry to have bothered you. I just happened to be out of change.
(*The gentleman approaches and offers* JIRŌ *his card.*)

SECRETARY

I have the honor, sir, to be your private secretary. The money I gave them was yours. With your permission, of course. I signed the check by authority. I gave them

10,000 yen plus a 2,000-yen gratuity. Really, it's becoming increasingly impossible these days to amuse oneself except on an expense account. They'll squeeze you out of every penny they can get. All they need to know is that our company is doing well for them to set their sights accordingly.

JIRŌ

Our company?

SECRETARY

Your company, sir, I mean, Mr. President.

JIRŌ

President?

SECRETARY

You mustn't pretend to be ignorant, sir! It's not kind of you. You seem to have a perverse streak, Mr. President.

JIRŌ

President? All right, have it your own way. I'd just as soon be a president. . . . Well then, prepare for me a detailed statement listing the capital of the firm as well as my personal property.

SECRETARY

Yes, sir. Immediately.
(*He signals to the right. A* FEMALE EMPLOYEE *wearing a suitable mask enters with a desk telephone and an account-book on a tray. She places the telephone next to* JIRŌ'S *pillow and the account-book in front of the* SECRETARY. *She then leaves.*)

JIRŌ

Read it aloud.

SECRETARY

Yes, sir.
(SECRETARY *puts on spectacles. The telephone rings. The* SECRETARY *answers it.*)

SECRETARY

Yes. Yes, sir. The president is here. (*covering the receiver with his hand*) It's that industrial firm in Osaka again. The usual matter.

JIRŌ

(*in an annoyed tone*) All right, all right. (*picking up the receiver*) Yes. I am. . . . I see. . . . Uh-huh . . . uh-huh . . . quite . . . oh . . . I see . . . Uh-huh . . . Really? . . . Well . . . Uh-huh . . . uh-huh . . . Ah-hah . . . I see. . . . I see. . . . I see. . . . I see. . . . Oh . . . Uh-huh . . . Uh-huh . . . Ah-hah . . . Good-bye (*hanging up*).

SECRETARY

You're the living image of the former president! You look exactly as he did on the telephone. That was just the way he used to get around a bothersome call. He was superb at it. You'd never hear a "yes" or a "no" from him. How wonderful to think his son has inherited his genius. No, there's no disputing blood. . . . It's strange, when I sit here like this I feel as if I were by his side again. . . . Ah, the memories that come back. (*He removes his glasses and looks up at the sky.*) As soon as he opened his eyes in the morning he would ring for me. I always used to spend a while every morning by his bedside inquiring about his plans for the day and answering the telephone. Then the newspaper would come. He liked the gossip column, and he would always read it after he finished the stock-market reports. Then, even that early in the morning, there would be his usual jokes—oh, dear—and next, his famous stewed chicken. He always ate stewed chicken for breakfast. People said that was why even when he was old he still retained his full powers. His stewed chicken was for a time very much in vogue in financial circles. No higher honor could have come to me than to have been permitted to partake of his stewed chicken. Every morning, with profound gratitude in my heart, I ate the gizzard and the tough parts of the liver. He ate only the soft parts, and I ate the rest. . . . Ah, those morning meals, how can I ever describe them. . . .

JIRŌ

Read me the accounts.

SECRETARY

(*putting on his glasses*) Yes, sir, immediately.
(*The telephone rings.* JIRŌ *answers it.*)

JIRŌ

Yes, it is. . . . Uh-huh . . . Mumble-mumble . . . Hah-hah . . . Well . . . Really? . . . Uh-huh . . . Good-bye.

SECRETARY

(*bowing*) Splendid! Splendid!

JIRŌ

How about the account?

SECRETARY

Yes, sir. . . .
(*Telephone rings.* SECRETARY *answers.*)

SECRETARY

Yes. Yes, it is. (*gesturing to* JIRŌ *to indicate that the call is from a woman*) Yes, he is (*passing receiver to* JIRŌ).

JIRŌ

Yes, it's me. You shouldn't bother me so early in the morning. I'm busy. I'm sick of your complaints. . . . Well, what do you know? Some people cry on the telephone! You should be ashamed of yourself. . . . We're through, as of today. . . . Yes. This is final. . . . I'll send some money later with my secretary. You understand me, don't you? (*He hangs up.*)

SECRETARY

Splendidly done. You did well to make a stand. You acted with true resolution. All I can say, sir, is that the former president must be rejoicing in his grave. To tell the truth, though it's hardly in my place to offer you advice, I must confess that I was rather disturbed about this matter, but you have disposed of it most forcefully. Yours is a truly illustrious nature!

JIRŌ

And now may I have the account?

SECRETARY

Yes, sir. I was so carried away. . . . The capital of the firm, as you know, is 230,000,000 yen. . . . Fixed assets are . . .

JIRŌ

How much of the stock do I hold?

SECRETARY

Yes, sir. Let me see—(*He turns the pages.*)

CHORUS

(*Noise of shouts and groans.*)

JIRŌ

What was that?

CHORUS

(*As before.*)

SECRETARY

It's not worth troubling yourself over, sir. The union is agitating about something.

CHORUS

(*As before.*)

JIRŌ

Quite a lot of noise for one union to make.

CHORUS

(*As before.*)

SECRETARY

(*looking behind him*) You're right, sir. The populace is also in agitation.

CHORUS

(*As before.*)

JIRŌ

How many shares have I?

SECRETARY

You own fifty-five per cent.

JIRŌ

(*dropping his head back toward the pillow*) Dispose of them all!

SECRETARY

Yes, sir!

JIRŌ

All of them, you hear me!

SECRETARY

This will create quite a sensation at the board and at the stockholders' meeting.

JIRŌ

Before we get to that, what are my personal assets?

SECRETARY

Eight million yen in real estate, twelve million yen in securities—of course we've done a good bit of juggling of accounts for income-tax purposes—for a total of twenty million yen.

JIRŌ

Dispose of all of them first.

SECRETARY

Mr. President, please be sure what you're doing.

CHORUS

(*As before.*)

JIRŌ

Divide all my assets among the union. The rest of my fortune is to be contributed to social work.

SECRETARY

There must be some profound reason behind this.

JIRŌ

There isn't any reason. I'm just sleepy. I want to go to sleep. That's all.
(*He turns his back to the audience and goes to sleep.*)

SECRETARY

(*to himself*) Ah-ha, I understand. He's got political ambitions. (*carrying the telephone over to the toy table at right*) Hello . . . hello . . . Is this the *Japan News?* Is Mr. Noyama there? The one who runs the political column in the city section . . . (*to himself*) I must help the president get started on his political career, though it means wearing myself to the bone, though it costs me my life. . . . Hello, Noyama? I've got big news for you. . . . Yes, it's hot. . . . The president of my company is turning over his entire fortune to the union and social works. He's going to found a new political party, without a penny. . . . Yes . . . Please give it suitable coverage. I'll be calling on you in the next day or so. . . . Please . . . Yes . . . Please, in just that way.

(*The scene becomes dark. The* SECRETARY *leaves. The* CHORUS sings the same song that accompanied the BEAUTY'S *entrance. It becomes light. Two men in the masks of old* GENTLEMEN *are standing facing right.*)

FIRST GENTLEMAN

It's a complete reversal.

SECOND GENTLEMAN

It certainly is.

FIRST GENTLEMAN

A kind of *coup d'état.*

SECOND GENTLEMAN

We've really been done in properly. It's less a *coup d'état* than a massacre.

FIRST GENTLEMAN

Not three years have gone by since he tossed away his fortune to enter politics. . . .

SECOND GENTLEMAN

Looking back on it now, that was what we should have done.

FIRST GENTLEMAN

But even supposing a poor man like myself wanted to throw away all his money—there's a limit to what he could throw.

SECOND GENTLEMAN

You always say that, but I'll bet you've got a fortune hidden away inside the family well.

FIRST GENTLEMAN

I have better uses for the family well than for hiding my money. That's where I intend to hide myself if the going gets rough.

SECOND GENTLEMAN

At our age it's degrading to be afraid of death. I always carry poison with me, wherever I go. It's part of a politician's personal equipment these days. (*He proudly displays the poison to* FIRST GENTLEMAN. *The latter examines the vial attentively. During the ensuing conversation it is placed on the table where it is forgotten.)*

FIRST GENTLEMAN

It's all over, now that the military clique is in his control.

SECOND GENTLEMAN

It's no wonder. The military leaders are at the beck and call of his party.

FIRST GENTLEMAN

It's simple enough to become a hero. Any man can become one, provided he has no desires. You can get more power and profit through indifference than through greed. Just imagine—in times like these a mere stripling can take over the country, just because he acts indifferent and claims—apparently in sincerity—not to need money, women, or fame.

SECOND GENTLEMAN

How would it be if you acted indifferent?

FIRST GENTLEMAN

It's too late.

SECOND GENTLEMAN

It's good you're aware of that, at least.

FIRST GENTLEMAN

However—

SECOND GENTLEMAN

I beg to inform you, "however" is a word which can only be used by intellectuals. It is not a politician's word.

FIRST GENTLEMAN

You've become a great fault-finder. It can't be helped, I suppose. However—as I was saying—now that he's got the military in his grip, runs parliament to suit himself, and is leader of the youth organizations, the next thing is war.

SECOND GENTLEMAN

Preparations have all been completed. Have you noticed how the tycoons of heavy industry have all been talking like patriots, of late? Just yesterday at the Industrialists' Club somebody gave a speech that was enough to make my head ache.

FIRST GENTLEMAN

They say the food is still good there.

SECOND GENTLEMAN

I can't stand the general leveling off of meals. It's bad for my kidneys if I don't eat a good meal once a week.

FIRST GENTLEMAN

It's surprising how dictators seem to prefer the most unappetizing food. They must feel they are serving the nation by torturing themselves. This one certainly sleeps late, considering how badly he eats.

SECOND GENTLEMAN

Other people make his plans for him while he sleeps. Then, when he wakes up, he makes speeches, still with that deathly pallor on his face. He acknowledges demonstrations, receives foreign envoys, and that's that.

FIRST GENTLEMAN

Everything is already under way.

SECOND GENTLEMAN

And the dictator is a sleepyhead.

FIRST GENTLEMAN

The program was thought up while he was asleep.

SECOND GENTLEMAN

That's a nice role, isn't it? The sleeping dictator. Even the day he came with his bodyguard they had to inject him with stimulants and he spent the whole night standing up, with his eyes big as saucers.

FIRST GENTLEMAN

Look! While our lord and master sleeps the streets have wakened and sprung to life.

SECOND GENTLEMAN

All those vulgar flags flying in the streets of this city where we grew up!

FIRST GENTLEMAN

Can you see how lovely the early morning clouds look? It's only since I've become old and get up early in the mornings that I've been able to appreciate them.

SECOND GENTLEMAN

I can't hear you. The youth groups have already started marching.

FIRST GENTLEMAN

A miserable state of affairs. Nowadays the young people get up earlier than the old.

(*A brass band, heard faintly at first, gradually grows louder.*)

CHORUS

Long live Jirō! Long live our Jirō!

FIRST GENTLEMAN

Our Jirō? What a dreadful state the world has come to!

CHORUS

Long live Jirō! Long live our Jirō!

FIRST GENTLEMAN

Once upon a time they used to say: "Long live the King!" What a falling off! The masses no longer have good taste.

CHORUS

Long live Jirō! Long live our Jirō!

FIRST GENTLEMAN

Just to hear those voices makes my rheumatism act up. Let's go smoke a cigar across the hall.

SECOND GENTLEMAN

Excellent idea. Until our leader, Jirō, deigns to open his eyes—eh? You have the cigars, I trust.

FIRST GENTLEMAN

No, I was hoping you would favor me with one of yours.

SECOND GENTLEMAN

Oh, did you? These days I can't afford such luxuries. (*They go out.*)

CHORUS

Long live Jirō! Long live our Jirō! (*The shouts fade into the distance. The brass band also fades out. The* CELEBRATED PHYSICIAN *enters. He wears a black cloak. Two* DOCTORS *follow him. They sit around the toy table and begin a discussion.*)

PHYSICIAN

Hush. Our leader is still asleep.

FIRST DOCTOR

He's still asleep.

SECOND DOCTOR

He's still asleep.

PHYSICIAN

While he's asleep we must make an important decision. I will shut my eyes and grope for one. Is it agreed? . . . I've touched something.

BOTH DOCTORS

He's touched something.

PHYSICIAN

(*Opens his eyes and looks. It is the vial left by the two gentlemen.*) It's poison!

BOTH DOCTORS

It's poison!

PHYSICIAN

It would appear, after all, that the eventuality which I have viewed with such apprehension is not to be avoided. As you undoubtedly are aware, I am a believer in what is known as the accident method of medical treatment, and I should be much obliged to you gentlemen for your concurrence. In brief—I omit detailed scientific explanations —I am convinced of the validity of the hypothesis that, in cases of extreme risk, it is scientific to rely on accidental indications. This method enables the physician to determine in advance by the laws of probability the success or failure of treatment. Just now, entirely by accident, my hand touched this poison which somehow happened to have been left here. According to my theory, this means that the only thing the patient before us requires is poison.

FIRST DOCTOR

It's most unlikely that in anything you would say you could be mistaken.

SECOND DOCTOR

All of the graduates of the Faculty of Medicine of this University will support your opinion as a golden rule.

PHYSICIAN

Gentlemen, a lamentable situation has arisen. Our Jirō, our leader, must take the poison. This is the situation with which we are faced.

FIRST DOCTOR

(*conferring with* SECOND DOCTOR) A most scientific opinion, I should say.

SECOND DOCTOR

Beyond any question of a doubt. Our academic traditions are not to be swayed by political considerations.

PHYSICIAN

Gentlemen, I am delighted from the bottom of my heart that you have favored me with your confidence. Our fatherland is soon to have recourse to action. At such a time a sleeping leader has no further mission. Indeed, from the moment he first appeared in the political world until today, this very day, our leader has been sleeping uninterruptedly. The only ones familiar with this secret, this great national secret, are myself and two or three others charged with affairs of state. A number of substitutes have always—mark you, always—functioned in his stead, and they have striven to maintain the leader's political power. The nation might be compared to a rich woman who goes to a party wearing an exact imitation of the diamond necklace she keeps locked up in the vault.

FIRST DOCTOR

Hear! hear!

SECOND DOCTOR

Your youthful ardor will serve us as an undying inspiration.

PHYSICIAN

The time for masquerades and imposture is at an end. Our fatherland is about to strike, and the groaning machinery has already begun to move forward. The wellspring of our strength is not our leader, or those near him, but the young people—the power of young people united together.

FIRST DOCTOR

Fascinating!

SECOND DOCTOR

He has the true fervor of the scientist.

PHYSICIAN

The machinery has already begun to move into action. We have no need of a sleeping leader. The sleeping dictator must die.

(*The two* DOCTORS *applaud.* JIRŌ *awakens and sits up in bed.*)

JIRŌ

What's all this? What's happening? Tell me, you, old man.

PHYSICIAN

This is the hour of our leader's death. We have permitted those closest to him to be present.
(*The* BEAUTY *and the three* DANCERS *enter. They are attired in black and their eyes are downcast. The* PRIVATE SECRETARY *also enters. All sit in reverent postures around the bed.*)

JIRŌ

This is certainly funny. What's the matter with everybody? Why is everybody suddenly so silent? Hey. (*poking one of the dancing girls*) Well, what do you know? She's crying. What's so sad? Crazy people.

PHYSICIAN

We have come to say good-bye to our leader.
(*They all prostrate themselves.*)

JIRŌ

You've all become so damned quiet again. Hey, what's the matter with you, my dear wife and lily blossom? I'm sorry I killed the baby.

PHYSICIAN

Some water, in a glass.

FIRST DOCTOR

Yes, sir.

PHYSICIAN

Please take this medicine.

JIRŌ

What *is* this medicine?

PHYSICIAN

Please drink it up bravely. We're all watching over your last moments.

JIRŌ

I don't want to. This is no joke. I don't wish to die.

PHYSICIAN

I beg you not to carry on like a small child, but to meet your fate like a man.

JIRŌ

Persistent, aren't you? I told you I didn't want to die.

PHYSICIAN

These are our leader's dying moments. Please do not render them unseemly.

JIRŌ

I don't want to die. Why doesn't one of you stop him? Women are of no use, even at such a time.

PHYSICIAN

This is not the moment for you to be defaming women. Come, drain the glass without further ado.

JIRŌ

No. I absolutely refuse.

PHYSICIAN

In that case, it can't be helped. I see that I shall have to convince you that you must drink it and spare us a most unattractive scene. Will everyone kindly leave? Entrust this matter to me. I realize that you would like to be present at his last moments, but I must ask you to go. (*They all leave except the* CELEBRATED PHYSICIAN.) Now, are you listening to me, Jirō? I am going to persuade you. Listen to me quietly. We are spirits from the town of Kantan. I presume you know what that means. It is our fixed rule that everyone who sleeps on this pillow must gain enlightenment. In ancient times there was a man who dreamed through a whole lifetime while a bowl of gruel was being cooked for him, and this made him realize the meaninglessness of human life. The same thing is still happening today. Everybody has always meekly and obediently lived through a lifetime while he dreamed. All the sleepers have really lived their dreams. Therefore, in order to intensify their awareness of the futility of human existence when they awaken from their dreams, they are always offered an elixir of immortality—that's in the dream in which they become Emperor. It is my job to offer the elixir. The others have all obeyed the rules, but what about you? From the very outset you haven't even tried to live, have you? There's not a particle of normal human nature in you. Even in your dreams you've utterly and completely rejected life. I have been watching all the time.

JIRŌ

But surely, old man, we are free, even in our dreams. Whether we try to live or whether we try not to live— and that's none of your business, is it?

PHYSICIAN

Your attitude is not precisely a polite one.

JIRŌ

It doesn't bother me in the least whether it is or it isn't.

PHYSICIAN

But it bothers me. There's no way to make a madman like you understand the futility of human existence—in other words, I can't accomplish my duty. When things have reached such a pass I cannot possibly bring you back to life again. It would be a violation of my sacred duties.

JIRŌ

You can talk all day long, but I still don't want to die.

PHYSICIAN

Contradiction! A contradiction! Your argument lacks all logical consistency.

JIRŌ

Why?

PHYSICIAN

Because you've never once tried to live. You've been dying while you're still alive. How can you say that you don't want to die?

JIRŌ

Nevertheless, I want to live.

PHYSICIAN

Please drink this first and then think about such idiocies.

JIRŌ

No! I want to live.
(JIRŌ, *who has been watching for the chance, suddenly snatches the poison from the* CELEBRATED PHYSICIAN, *and dashes it to the ground. The old man disappears with a cry. The stage becomes dark. After a pause the* shōji *gradually grows faintly white, and it is possible to see* JIRŌ *sleeping as before. The* shōji *continues to grow lighter. There is a tumultuous twittering of birds outside in the garden.* KIKU *enters. She wakens* JIRŌ *by shaking his shoulders.*)

KIKU

Please wake up, young master.

JIRŌ

Umm. Umm.

KIKU

Wake up, please. Ah, you were sleeping with such an innocent face. Just as you used to, when you were a baby.

JIRŌ

Umm. Umm.

KIKU

Please do get up. Breakfast is ready now. The rice is steaming hot. You always used to say that you wouldn't eat rice unless Kiku had cooked it.

JIRŌ

It's morning, is it?

KIKU

Broad daylight. The weather is wonderful.

JIRŌ

Kiku, I've had the most amazing dreams.

KIKU

(*uneasily, lowering her voice*) I suppose . . .

JIRŌ

"I suppose"? No, you're mistaken. I'm a little different from the others. Life is just what I thought it was. Nothing surprised me at all.

KIKU

If you're going off, like my husband . . .

JIRŌ

You wish I would, I suppose. You'd like me to go off wandering.
(KIKU *is silent.*)

JIRŌ

You'll have to resign yourself—forget about your husband. I'm not going anywhere. You've lost your chance of coming along with me. You've lost the chance of meeting your husband.

KIKU

It makes me feel so relieved and strong to hear you say that. It's strange.

JIRŌ

That feeling is true, Kiku—you're alive.

KIKU

Young master, are you really going to stay here all the time and not leave me?

JIRŌ

I certainly will. All the time. You don't mind, do you?

KIKU

I'm so happy. This room served a purpose after all. I feel so happy to think that I'll be able to stay with the young master, just the two of us. I feel as if the Kiku of ten years ago has returned to life.

JIRŌ

I'll remain here all the time. Perhaps until I die.

KIKU

I shall forget about my husband. I feel as if life here somehow will be entirely new. Why is it, I wonder? I feel as if there's never been such an exhilarating morning.

JIRŌ

(*Stands, opens the* shōji *a little, and steps out on the verandah.*) Oh-h, it's pretty. Kiku, the whole garden is full of flowers. (*Incessant chirping of birds.*)

KIKU

The flowers have bloomed?

JIRŌ

(*from the garden*) Look! Lilies, roses, violets, primroses, asters. It's beautiful. They've all bloomed at once!

KIKU

(*peeping from the opening between the panels of the* shōji) It's unbelievable! Who would have thought such a morning would come?

JIRŌ

(*his voice is far off*) Kiku, where's the well for washing?

KIKU

Over there. To the left.

JIRŌ

(*very far off*) It's full of flowers, all around the well.

KIKU

It's strange . . . it's strange. The garden has come back to life.

CURTAIN

THE LADY AOI

CHARACTERS:

YASUKO ROKUJŌ

HIKARU WAKABAYASHI

AOI

NURSE

❁ *A ROOM in a hospital. It is late at night. To stage-right is a large window draped with a curtain. At the back, a bed in which* AOI *is sleeping. To the left is a door.*

HIKARU

(*Enters, led in by the* NURSE. *He wears a raincoat and is carrying a suitcase. He is an unusually good-looking man. He speaks in an undertone.*) She's asleep, isn't she?

NURSE

Yes, she's sound asleep.

HIKARU

It won't waken her if I talk in a normal voice, will it?

NURSE

You can talk a little bit louder if you wish. The medicine is taking effect.

HIKARU

(*looking down intently at* AOI's *face*) How peaceful she looks as she sleeps.

NURSE

Her face looks peaceful enough now.

HIKARU

Now?

NURSE

Yes, but late at night . . .

HIKARU

She's in pain?

NURSE

In terrible pain.

HIKARU

(*reading the chart at the foot of the bed*) "Aoi Wakabayashi. Admitted at 9 p.m. on the 12th." . . . I wonder if there's anywhere I might spend the night here.

NURSE

Yes. (*She points to the left-rear.*) In the next room.

HIKARU

Is there bedding and all?

NURSE

Yes, there is. Would you like to lie down now?

HIKARU

No, I'll stay up a bit longer. (*He sits on the chair, lights a cigarette.*) I was on a business trip when I got word she was sick. They said it was nothing serious. But when somebody gets put in the hospital it must be serious, mustn't it?

NURSE

Your wife has often had attacks like this, hasn't she?

HIKARU

It's not the first time. But it was a very important business trip. I managed this morning to get through my work and I rushed back as fast as I could. Being away made me worry all the more.

NURSE

I'm sure it did.
(*The telephone on the table tinkles faintly.*)

HIKARU

(*lifting the receiver to his ear*) I can't hear anything.

NURSE

It often rings that way about this time of night.

HIKARU

It's out of order, I suppose. But why should there be a telephone in a hospital room?

NURSE

Every room in this hospital has a telephone.

HIKARU

Who would want to telephone a sick man?

NURSE

It's for the patients' use. There aren't enough nurses to go round, and we ask the patients to call for one on the inside line in case of an emergency. Or, supposing a patient would like a book, he can telephone the bookshop himself. That's on the outside line. We have three operators working twenty-four hours a day in shifts to take care of the outside line. Of course, when patients require absolute quiet, no calls are accepted.

HIKARU

And isn't my wife absolutely quiet?

NURSE

She tosses around a good deal after she falls asleep. She lifts her arms, groans, moves her body from side to side. You really can't say she's absolutely quiet.

HIKARU

(*getting angry*) You mean to say, in this hospital . . .

NURSE

In this hospital we accept no responsibility for the dreams of our patients.
(*Pause. The* NURSE *shows signs of restlessness.*)

HIKARU

What are you so nervous about?

NURSE

It's not necessarily because I've been attracted by you.

HIKARU

(*laughing in spite of himself*) This hospital seems crazier every minute.

NURSE

You're a very good-looking man, you know. A real Prince Genji. But the discipline for nurses in this hospital is terribly strict. We've all been under psychoanalysis, and our sex complexes have all been cleared up. (*She spreads open her arms.*) *All* of them. Things are arranged so we can always satisfy our demands. The director of the hospital and the young doctors are very competent in this respect. Whenever necessary they administer the medicine as prescribed, the medicine known as sex. We never have any trouble with one another.

HIKARU

(*impressed*) You don't say?

NURSE

So, you see, it's perfectly obvious to all of us, without having to make any special analysis, that your wife's dreams all result from sexual complexes. There's nothing for you to worry about. She should be placed under analysis so she can be freed from her complexes. We're giving her the sleep treatment as a first step.

HIKARU

You mean, my wife, with this sleep treatment . . .

NURSE

Yes. (*still fidgeting*) That's why I can't have the least of what they call "understanding" for the patients or, if you'll excuse me, the patients' families or visitors. Don't you agree? Every last one of them is the ghost of a libido. Even that strange visitor who comes here every night . . .

HIKARU

Every night? Here? A visitor?

NURSE

Oh—now I've said it. It's been going on every night, ever since your wife entered the hospital. And it's always late, around this time, because the visitor isn't free any earlier. I've been strictly forbidden to mention it, but it came out before I knew it. . . .

HIKARU

Is it a man—this visitor?

NURSE

Please set your mind at ease—it's a middle-aged woman, a very beautiful one. . . . She'll be coming any minute now. When she arrives I always take advantage of her visit to go out and rest for a while. I don't know why it is, but it makes me feel oddly depressed to be near her.

HIKARU

What sort of woman is she?

NURSE

A very stylishly dressed lady. The upper bourgeoisie—that's the impression she gives. You know, surprisingly enough, it's in bourgeois families that you find the worst sexual repressions. . . . Anyway, she'll be here before long. (*She walks to window at right, raises the curtain.*) Look. There's hardly a house left with its lights burning. All you can see are the two sharp lines of the street lamps. Now is the hour of love. Of loving, of fighting, of hating. When the daytime combat ends, the war by night begins, a gorier, more abandoned struggle. The bugles of the night that proclaim the outbreak of hostilities are sounding now. A woman sheds blood, dies, and comes back to life time and time again. And she must always die once before she can live. These men and women who fight wear black badges of morning over their weapons. Their flags are all pure white, but trampled on, wrinkled, and sometimes stained with blood. The drummer is beating his drum, the drum of the heart, the drum of honor and shame. . . . How gently they breathe, they who are about to die. Look at them die, brazenly flaunting their wounds, the gaping, fatal wounds. Some men go to death with their faces in the mire. Shame is the decoration they wear. Look. It's not surprising you can't see any lights. What lie before you, row on row, as far as the eye can see, are not houses but graves, foul, putrefied graves. The light of the moon will never glitter on those granite slabs. . . . We're angels compared to them. We stand aloof from the world of love, from the hour of love. All we do, and that only occasionally, is to produce in bed a chemical change. No matter how many hospitals like this there may be, there aren't enough. The director always says so. . . .

Oh, she's come. She's come! In that car she always rides in, a big silvery car. It will race here as if it's on wings, and pull up smartly in front of the hospital. Look! (HIKARU *goes to the window.*) It's going over the viaduct now. It always comes from that direction. There—you see—it's taking the long way round. . . . Oh, it's here already, in front of the hospital, before it seems possible. The door of the car has been opened. I'll be leaving you. Good night. (*She bolts precipitately from the room by the door to the left. Pause. The telephone gives forth a faint, choked tinkle. Pause. From the door to the left appears the living phantasm of* YASUKO ROKUJŌ. *She is dressed in Japanese clothes of an expensive cut. She wears black gloves.*)

HIKARU

Mrs. Rokujō!

MRS. ROKUJŌ

Hikaru! What a long time it's been, hasn't it?

HIKARU

So it was you, the visitor in the middle of the night.

MRS. ROKUJŌ

Who told you about it? (HIKARU *does not reply*) It must have been that nurse. She's such a chatterbox. . . . You know, I've not been coming here to pay a sick-call—it's been to deliver flowers, every night, on your behalf, ever since I heard you were away.

HIKARU

Flowers?

MRS. ROKUJŌ

(*She opens her hands.*) No, there's nothing in my hands. My flowers are invisible. Flowers of pain is what they are. (*She pretends to arrange flowers at the head of* AOI's *bed.*) These buds I arrange by her pillow will open into ash-colored blossoms. Many horrible thorns are hidden underneath the leaves, and the flowers themselves exude a loathsome odor that will permeate the room. Look, the peaceful expression drains from her face; the cheeks tremble and are filled with dread. (*She holds her gloved hands over* AOI's *face.*) Aoi is dreaming now that her face has become hideous to look at. The face she had always thought beautiful when she saw it in her mirror has turned into a mass of wrinkles—that is what she dreams. If now I gently touch my hand to her throat (*she touches the sick woman's throat*) Aoi will dream she is being strangled. A rush of blood comes to her face, the breath is choked, her hands and feet writhe in anguish.

HIKARU

(*pushing* MRS. ROKUJŌ's *hand aside in consternation*) What are you doing to Aoi?

MRS. ROKUJŌ

(*She moves away. Speaks gently, from a distance.*) I am trying to make her suffer.

HIKARU

Excuse me, but Aoi is my wife, and I won't permit you to bother her any further. Please be so good as to leave.

MRS. ROKUJŌ

(*even gentler*) I will not leave.

HIKARU

What do you—

MRS. ROKUJŌ

(*She approaches and gently takes* HIKARU'*s hand.*) I came tonight because I wanted to see you.

HIKARU

(*He wrests away his hand.*) Your hand is like ice.

MRS. ROKUJŌ

That's not surprising. There's no blood in it.

HIKARU

Those gloves of yours . . .

MRS. ROKUJŌ

If you dislike my gloves I'll remove them. Nothing could be simpler. (*She slips off her gloves as she walks across the room, and puts them next to the telephone.*) At any rate, I have business, important business, that must be disposed of. That's why I have been running about this way—don't think it hasn't been a nuisance—in the middle of the night. The middle of the night . . . (*She looks at her wristwatch.*) It's already after one. The night is not like the day, it's free. All things, people and inanimate objects alike, sleep. This wall, the chest of drawers, the window panes, the door—all of them are asleep. And while they sleep they're full of cracks and crevices—it's no problem to pass through them. When you pass through a wall not even the wall is aware of it. What do you suppose night is? Night is when all things are in harmony. By day light and shadow war, but with nightfall the night inside the house holds hands with the night outside the house. They are the same thing. The night air is party to the conspiracy. Hate and love, pain and joy: everything and anything join hands in the night air. The murderer in the dark, I am sure, feels affection for the woman he has killed. (*Laughs.*) What is it? Why do you stare at me that way? You must be shocked to see what an old woman I've become.

HIKARU

I thought you swore never to see me again.

MRS. ROKUJŌ

You were very happy to hear me make that vow. Then you married Aoi. (*She turns fiercely at the sleeping* AOI.) This weak, sickly woman! (*emptily*) Since then every night has been sleepless. Even when I shut my eyes I have not slept. I have not slept a wink since then.

HIKARU

Have you come here to be pitied by me?

MRS. ROKUJŌ

I really don't know myself why I've come. When I feel I want to kill you, I must be thinking that I'd like to be pitied by your dead self. And amidst feelings of every sort, simultaneously, there is myself. Isn't it strange that I should be present at the same time with all those different existences?

HIKARU

I don't understand what you're talking about.

MRS. ROKUJŌ

(*lifting her face to his*) Kiss me.

HIKARU

Stop it, please.

MRS. ROKUJŌ

Your beautiful eyebrows, your terrifyingly clear eyes, your cold nose, your——

HIKARU

Stop it, please.

MRS. ROKUJŌ

——your lips. (*She kisses him quickly.*)

HIKARU

(*jumping back*) Stop it, please, I say.

MRS. ROKUJŌ

The first time I kissed you, too, you shied away like a deer, just as you did now.

HIKARU

Yes, I did. I wasn't particularly in love with you. All I had was a childish curiosity. You took advantage of it. I suppose you've learned now the punishment a woman gets for taking advantage of a man's curiosity.

MRS. ROKUJŌ

You were not the least in love. You studied me. That, at least, was your intent, wasn't it? How adorable you were! I hope you'll always stay that way!

HIKARU

I'm not a child any more. I am in fact the head of a household. Have you no sense of shame? That's my wife who's sleeping there next to you.

MRS. ROKUJŌ

My only purpose in coming here has been to dispose of my business. I have nothing to be ashamed of.

HIKARU

What business have you?

MRS. ROKUJŌ

To be loved by you.

HIKARU

Are you in your right mind, Mrs. Rokujō?

MRS. ROKUJŌ

My name is Yasuko.

HIKARU

I am not obliged to call you by your first name.

MRS. ROKUJŌ

(*Suddenly kneels, throws her arms around* HIKARU's *knees, and rubs her cheek against them.*) I beg you, please don't be so cold to me.

HIKARU

This is the first time I've ever seen you lose your pride so. (*to himself*) It's funny. It doesn't feel as if a human being were holding me, and yet I can't move my feet.

MRS. ROKUJŌ

I had no pride, from the very beginning.

HIKARU

You should have confessed it earlier. Perhaps things might have lasted awhile longer.

MRS. ROKUJŌ

It was your fault not to have realized it. Couldn't you tell that my eyes had long since lost their pride? The clearest sign that a woman has lost her pride is when she talks in a highhanded way. A woman longs to be a queen because a queen has the most pride to lose. . . . Ah, your knees—your knees are a cold, hard pillow.

HIKARU

Yasuko . . .

MRS. ROKUJŌ

I could sleep on this pillow. A cold, hard pillow that would never get warm. . . . My pillow becomes scalding hot as soon as my head touches it, and my head spends the night fleeing from the pillow's heat to the cold. A man who could walk barefoot over burning desert sands could not tread on my pillow.

HIKARU

(*somewhat gentler*) Please be careful. I am a very weak man when my pity is aroused.

MRS. ROKUJŌ

Now I understand! You married Aoi out of pity too! Didn't you?

HIKARU

(*pushing her aside*) Don't jump to any conclusions like that. (*He sits on the chair.* MRS. ROKUJŌ *still clings to his legs and rubs her cheek against his knees like a cat.*)

MRS. ROKUJŌ

Please don't abandon me.

HIKARU

(*smoking*) You were abandoned long ago.

MRS. ROKUJŌ

You still love me.

HIKARU

Did you come here to tell me that? (*teasingly*) I thought you said you came to torture Aoi.

MRS. ROKUJŌ

I was aiming to kill two birds with one stone. Give me a cigarette, please. (HIKARU *offers her one, but* MRS. ROKUJŌ *snatches the half-smoked cigarette from* HIKARU'S *mouth and puffs at it.* HIKARU, *at a loss what else to do, puts the cigarette he had offered her into his mouth and lights it.*)

HIKARU

In those days I was unstable, shaky on my feet. I wanted to be chained. I wanted a cage to shut me in. You were that cage. Then, when I wished to be free again, you were still a cage, a chain.

MRS. ROKUJŌ

I loved to look at your eyes, those eyes searching for freedom inside the cage that was myself, the chain that was myself. That was when I first really fell in love with you. It was autumn, the beginning of autumn. You had come to visit me at my house on the lake. I went to meet you in my sailboat, as far as the yacht harbor next to the station.

. . . It was a wonderfully clear day. The mast was creaking gently. The boat . . .

HIKARU

The sail above the boat . . .

MRS. ROKUJŌ

(*with sudden asperity*) Don't you find it disagreeable to share the same memories with me?

HIKARU

They're not the same. We happened to have been together, that's all.

MRS. ROKUJŌ

But it was the same boat. The sail was flapping madly above us. Oh, if that sail were here again! If only it stood over us again!

HIKARU

(*staring at the window*) Is that it coming from out there?

MRS. ROKUJŌ

It's come!

(*Weird music. From the right a large sailboat glides onstage. It moves forward with the deliberation of a swan, and halts between them and the bed, where it stands like a screen shielding the bed.* HIKARU *and* MRS. ROKUJŌ *act as if they were aboard the boat.*)

MRS. ROKUJŌ

We're on the lake!

HIKARU

A wonderful breeze!

MRS. ROKUJŌ

This is the first time you've come to my country house, isn't it? It's on the side of the lake below the mountain. Soon you'll be able to see the roof, behind that clump of trees. It's a pale-green roof. Foxes prowl around the house when it gets dark, you know, and you can hear them yelping in the mountains. Have you every heard a fox's cries?

HIKARU

No, never.

MRS. ROKUJŌ

Tonight you'll hear them. And the shrieks that a chicken lets out before it dies, when a fox is ripping its throat.

HIKARU

I'd just as soon not hear such things.

MRS. ROKUJŌ

I'm sure you'll like my garden, I'm sure of it. In the spring parsley grows along the borders of the lawn and fills the garden with the most delicious scent. Then, when the spring rains fall, the garden becomes submerged and completely disappears. You can see the hydrangea blossoms drowning as the water creeps up through the grass. Have you ever seen a drowned hydrangea? It's autumn now and swarms of tiny insects will be flying up from the reeds in the garden to skim over the surface of the lake, like sleds on the ice.

HIKARU

That's your house over there, isn't it?

MRS. ROKUJŌ

Yes, the one with the pale-green roof. You can tell it from much farther off in the evening, because of the sunset. The roof and the windows sparkle, and the light is like a beacon that tells from afar where the house is. (*Pause.*) What's the matter? You're not saying a word.

HIKARU

(*gently*) There's no need to say anything.

MRS. ROKUJŌ

It's medicine to me to hear you talk that way, a medicine that cures all my wounds in an instant, a marvelous medicine. But I know the kind of person you are—you give the medicine first and only afterward inflict the wound. You never do it the other way. First the medicine, after the medicine the wound, and after the wound no more medicine . . . I understand well enough. I'm already an old woman. Once I get wounded I won't recover quickly like a girl. I tremble with fright whenever you say anything affectionate. I wonder what horrible wound awaits me after so efficacious a medicine. Of late, the less affectionate you talk the happier it makes me.

HIKARU

You seem convinced that you're going to suffer.

MRS. ROKUJŌ

Pain comes, as night follows the day, sooner or later.

HIKARU

I can't believe I have the strength to cause anybody pain.

MRS. ROKUJŌ

That's because you're young. One of these days you will wake up in the morning with nothing on your mind, and while you are out walking with your dog, perhaps, you will suddenly become aware that dozens of women somewhere, unseen by you, are suffering, and you will understand that the very fact you are alive is in itself a cause of suffering to many women. Even though you can't see them, they can see you, and it is useless for you to turn your eyes away, for you are as plainly visible as a castle that rises on a height over a city.

HIKARU

Why don't we drop the subject?

MRS. ROKUJŌ

Yes, let's. As long as I can still talk about such things I should count myself lucky.

HIKARU

I can see your house very clearly now—the latticework of the second-floor windows, the wooden railing of the balcony. There's nobody at home, is there?

MRS. ROKUJŌ

No, the house is empty. That's where I'd like to live with you until I die.

HIKARU

Until you die? You shouldn't talk of such uncertainties. Who knows—we may die tomorrow. Supposing, for example, the boat capsized . . .

MRS. ROKUJŌ

The boat capsized! I wonder why I didn't buy a boat for you which would instantly capsize? Obviously I hadn't my wits about me.

HIKARU

(*shaking the mast*) Look! It's going to turn over!
(MRS. ROKUJŌ *throws her arms around* HIKARU. *They embrace.*)

AOI'S VOICE

(*faintly, from the distance*) Help! Help!
(*As her voice is heard, the shadow of* AOI, *writhing on her sickbed with her arms thrust out, appears on the sail.*)

HIKARU

Wasn't that a voice somewhere just now?

MRS. ROKUJŌ

No, it must have been a fox. In the daytime, when the lake is still, you can hear the fox yelps gliding over the water, all the way from the mountain.

HIKARU

I can't hear it any more.

MRS. ROKUJŌ

I wonder why there must be a left and a right to everything. Now I am standing by your right side. That means your heart is far away. But if I move to your left side I won't be able to see your right profile.

HIKARU

The only thing for me to do is to turn into a gas and evaporate.

MRS. ROKUJŌ

Yes. When I am on your right I am jealous of everything to your left. I feel as if someone surely is sitting there.

HIKARU

(*He makes the motions of leaning over the side of the boat and dipping his hand in the water.*) The lake's the only thing sitting on my left. What a cold hand it has! . . . Look at that! (*He shows her his wet hand.*) It's almost frozen. And it's only the beginning of autumn.
(*There is a groan behind the sail.*)

HIKARU

What was that?

MRS. ROKUJŌ

What?

HIKARU

I couldn't hear. It sounded as if someone were groaning.

MRS. ROKUJŌ

(*She listens intently.*) It's the creaking of the mast.

HIKARU

The wind has shifted, hasn't it? (*He makes the gestures of manipulating the sail.*) I see the reeds on the shore plainly now, bending in the wind. The wind is shaking spasms over the surface of the lake.

MRS. ROKUJŌ

Yes, isn't it? . . . I was just thinking that, if you fell in love with some woman much younger and prettier than I, and you married her . . .

HIKARU

Yes?

MRS. ROKUJŌ

I don't think I would die.

HIKARU

(*Laughs.*) That's fine.

MRS. ROKUJŌ

I wouldn't die, but I think I would certainly kill her. My spirit would leave my body even while I was still alive, and it would go to torture her. My living ghost would afflict her and torment her and torture her, and it would not cease until it killed her. She, poor creature, would die haunted night after night by an evil spirit.

AOI'S VOICE

(*faintly, from the distance*) Help! Help!

HIKARU

That voice again. What can it be?

MRS. ROKUJŌ

It's just the sail flapping in the wind. It's the sound of the wind.

(*The shadow-image of* AOI *thrusting out her arms in anguish is clearly projected on the sail.*)

AOI'S VOICE

(*fairly loudly this time*) Ah-h! Ah-h! Help! Help!

HIKARU

(*aghast*) I'm sure I heard a voice.

MRS. ROKUJŌ

It was the shriek of a chicken whose windpipe was gnawed by a fox. The wind carried it here from the shore. That shows how close we are.

HIKARU

I wonder if someone isn't drowning.

MRS. ROKUJŌ

Drowning? Who would be drowning? If anyone's drowning, it's us!

AOI'S VOICE

(*clearly*) Help! Help!

HIKARU

It's Aoi!

MRS. ROKUJŌ

(*Laughs.*) No, it's a chicken.

HIKARU

I'm sure it's Aoi's voice.

MRS. ROKUJŌ

Don't leave me!

HIKARU

You're responsible! You've been torturing Aoi.

MRS. ROKUJŌ

No, it's not my fault. It's your—

AOI'S VOICE

(*Groans.*)

HIKARU

Aoi!

MRS. ROKUJŌ

Try to get hold of yourself! You're not in love with Aoi. Look at me. Make no mistake. You're in love with me. With me.

HIKARU

(*Shakes his head.*) No, I am not.
(*The two confront each other in silence. Weird music.* MRS. ROKUJŌ *turns from* HIKARU *and attempts to pass behind the sail.* HIKARU *stops her.* MRS. ROKUJŌ *twists herself free and disappears behind the sail.* HIKARU *follows her. The stage becomes dark. Amidst weird music the sailboat slowly moves offstage to the left. When it is no longer visible the stage becomes light again.* MRS. ROKUJŌ *is not to be seen.* HIKARU *stands alone in apparent stupefaction.*)

HIKARU

(*As if struck by a sudden thought, he picks up the telephone receiver on the desk.*) Hello, hello. Yes. Outside line, please. . . . Is this outside? Please give me Nakano 999. . . . Hello. Is that Mr. Rokujō's house? May I speak to Yasuko? Yes, Mrs. Rokujō. . . . She retired some time ago? Yes? In her bedroom? . . . I'm sorry, it can't be helped. Please wake her. Tell her Hikaru is calling. It's urgent. Please wake her. Yes. . . .
(*Pause.* HIKARU *looks anxiously at* AOI'*s bed. She is sleeping peacefully in a supine position.*)

HIKARU

Hello, hello . . . Is that you, Yasuko? What? Have you been at home all evening? You've been asleep? This *is*

Yasuko I'm talking with, isn't it? (*to himself*) Yes, the voice is certainly hers. . . . Then what I saw was a living ghost. . . . Yes, hello, hello.

(*There is a knock on the door to the left.*)

MRS. ROKUJŌ'S VOICE

(*from outside the door. She speaks very distinctly.*) Hikaru, I've forgotten something. I forgot my gloves. My black gloves, next to the telephone. Do you see them? Please get them for me.

(HIKARU *distractedly picks up the black gloves and, leaving the receiver off the hook, walks to the door to the left. He opens the door and goes out. As soon as* HIKARU *leaves,* MRS. ROKUJŌ'S *voice on the telephone suddenly becomes loud enough for the audience to hear.*)

MRS. ROKUJŌ'S VOICE

(*from the telephone*) Hello. Hello . . . What is it, Hikaru? What's the matter? You wake me up in the middle of the night, and then suddenly you don't say a word. What do you want? Why don't you answer? . . . Hello, Hikaru, hello, hello . . .

(*At the last "hello" from the telephone,* AOI *thrusts out her arms at the telephone and with a horrible cry collapses over the bed and dies. The stage immediately blacks* out.)

CURTAIN

HANJO

❁ *CHARACTERS:* HANAKO, *a mad girl*

JITSUKO HONDA, *a spinster*

YOSHIO, *a young man*

❀ JITSUKO HONDA's *atelier. Autumn. From afternoon to evening. The room is in disorder with evident preparations for a journey.* JITSUKO, *seated in an easy-chair, reads a newspaper. She puts down the newspaper, stands up impatiently, only to sit again and read.*

JITSUKO

(*to herself*) It's come to nothing, to nothing, all that I've been through. I could tear this newspaper to shreds. . . . But tearing it up would do no good. No, the best thing for me would be to read it aloud, the way people do, with animation and interest, as if it happened to someone else. I should read it in a manner befitting the esteemed daughter of a father who believes that his is the only household unvisited by human unhappiness and a mother who is convinced that her husband is the only man in the world, as a devoted daughter might read to her parents by way of entertainment after dinner. (*as if there are others present*) Generous Father, the richest man in town, Mother dear, your esteemed daughter, whom you still send money for her painting lessons and who is unmarried at forty, will now read you an interesting article. (*She reads.*) "Tragic love of mad girl. Old-fashioned romance at railway station . . . A beautiful mad girl may be seen every day, rain or shine, sitting on a bench in the waiting-room of a certain station with an opened fan in her arms. She peers into the face of every man who alights at the station, only to return each time disappointed to her bench. In reply to a reporter's questions she said that this was Hanjo's fan.[1] A man she met at a certain place exchanged fans with her as a pledge that they should meet again. The mad girl holds a man's fan with a snow scene painted on it. The faithless man has her fan with a moonflower design. The man has never returned, and the girl has gone mad with longing. Her name is Hanako, and, according to a station attendant, she lives at the house of the lady artist Miss Jitsuko Honda, at Number 35 X Street."

Living at the house of Miss Jitsuko Honda, did it say? All I've gone through up to now has been so much foam on the water. It was useless of me never to have submitted to an exhibition any of the pictures I painted of Hanako, preferring people not to see them. If I had submitted them, who knows, they might have been selected or even won prizes. But ever since I've known Hanako I've only sent the other pictures, the ones I didn't put myself into, and every time they have been rejected. And it has been for nothing. After all I have been through I thought that Hanako would never leave my hands. And in spite of that— (*She starts frantically cutting the newspaper with*

[1] Hanjo was the name of a Chinese court lady of ancient times whose fan was celebrated in poetry.

scissors into tiny snowflake-like fragments.) I suppose that it was fated to happen sooner or later. I could not bind Hanako to me. If I had tried, she would surely long since have faded into nothing, like a cricket one buys in the market and puts in a cage to give one pleasure for a couple of days. I had no choice but to do what I did.

Sooner or later people are bound now to start talking about the beautiful mad girl with the fan, and next it will come to the ears of Yoshio, that faithless creature. (*She rises wildly.*) The only thing is to go on a trip somewhere. The only thing to do is to run away without a moment's delay, for as long as possible, just the two of us, and hide until the sensation dies down. If he were utterly devoid of any feeling for her there would not be so much to be afraid of, but vanity may call him back, for all I know. We'll leave tonight. Nothing else can be done. Just the two of us, for some faraway place. . . . Then, if we are overtaken (*she laughs*) it won't matter much if I die. Yes, that will be quite all right. (*She begins again to make preparations for the journey.*)

(HANAKO *enters.*)

JITSUKO

(*pretending to be calm*) Oh, you're back already.

HANAKO

(*extremely beautiful but heavily made up, and over-dressed in a somewhat soiled costume. She holds against her breast, opened, a large fan with a snow scene painted on it.*) It will be all right, won't it, if I leave the door open? So that if Yoshio comes he can go right in.

JITSUKO

Yes, leave it open. For now— But winter is coming on.

HANAKO

It's autumn, isn't it. An autumn fan, an autumn fan, a fan for autumn. (*She weeps.*)

JITSUKO

(*putting her arms about* HANAKO's *shoulders*) There's no need to cry. Yoshio will surely come for you one day.

HANAKO

Today I waited again at the station, all day long, all day long. I think that I've come to life through waiting for him. I looked at the faces of the people getting off the train. None of them looked like his. They were all faces of other people. I don't think anyone has a living face except Yoshio. The faces of all the other men in the world are dead. They are all skeletons. Many, many people with skulls instead of heads and brief cases in their hands got off at the station. I was so tired. Jitsuko, I waited all day today, too.

JITSUKO

I have never once waited for anything.

HANAKO

It doesn't matter with you. There's no need for you to wait. But some people must wait. *My* body is filled with waiting. The evening dusk always comes to the moonflower and the morning to the morning-glory, but I wait,

I pine, yes, my body is filled with prickling pine needles. Don't they say that human beings go on living by waiting and making other people wait? If you gave your whole life to waiting, how would it be? (*She points to her body.*) Is this my body? Am I an unshut window? An unshut door? (*She points to the door.*) Like that door . . . Can I go on living without sleeping? Am I a doll that does not sleep?

JITSUKO

You are beautiful. I can't believe that there is anyone in the world more beautiful than you. Everybody opens many windows too widely, thinking to improve the ventilation, only to lose everything as a result. But you have only one window, and through that window everything in the world enters you. You are the richest person in the world.

HANAKO

(*She is not listening.*) Today, too, I sat all day on a wooden bench. How hard that bench is. I had intended waiting for him on soft grass. When he came I would jump up and he would brush my dress for me. "Oh, see how your dress is stained by the grass."

JITSUKO

I love to see you naked. I have never seen nakedness as pure and rich as yours. Your breasts, your belly, your thighs . . . It was worth waiting.

HANAKO

What do you say?

JITSUKO

Because you waited you possess all the beautiful things in the world. A woman somewhere one morning lost her breasts, and then they were shining on your body, like medals of flesh, wonderfully fragrant. What men have fought to win, you have won by waiting.

HANAKO

(*not listening*) Spring, summer, autumn . . . Which comes first, summer or autumn? If my fan were here now and the moonflowers alive, wouldn't summer come? (*playing with the fan, opening and shutting it*) How happy I'd be if the snowflakes in this design would suddenly melt away! (*She shuts the fan.*)

JITSUKO

Hanako, let's go on a trip.

HANAKO

(*shielding her face with an exaggerated gesture*) Why? Why?

JITSUKO

We'll go look for Yoshio. Why don't we leave as soon as possible, tonight even? You'll never find him by waiting that way. Let's go all through Japan looking for him. From village to village, from town to town, traveling, the two of us—how enjoyable it will be. Soon it will be the season for autumn leaves. The mountains will all turn crimson. I want to see how healthy you look when the autumn tints are reflected on the paleness of your face. If we go, I'll help you with all my heart to search for him. On the train I'll ask every young man if he is Yoshio.

HANAKO

No . . . no . . .

JITSUKO

Why don't you want to go?

HANAKO

Isn't it like running away from something?

JITSUKO

(*starting*) Running away?

HANAKO

It's because you don't wait, because you're a person who never waits. People who don't wait run away. I shall wait here. I won't listen to another word you say. Don't be angry, will you? If only I had stayed in the town where I met him and not gone away, he might have come again. But you dragged me here. . . . (*She notices the scraps of newspaper on the floor.*) What's this?

JITSUKO

(*paling*) It isn't anything.

HANAKO

It's snow! I'm sure it's snow. Dirty snow . . . (*For a few minutes she scoops up the paper, then scatters it around her.*) See! The snow has fallen. (*with the cunning *of the insane*) The snow has fallen, it's winter already. We don't have to go on any trip. Just pretend that we've been traveling since autumn, and now that winter's come we've returned.

JITSUKO

No, it's no use, Hanako, we must go away.

HANAKO

No, no.

JITSUKO

Do you understand? (*She pushes* HANAKO *into a chair, and leaning over her she speaks in a persuasive tone.*) You have waited long enough. You have waited enough and become so beautiful that if he should meet you he would never be able to leave you again. Do you understand? You must stop waiting and go to look for him.

HANAKO

No, I will not move from here. I will not move for the rest of my life. The world is so big that no matter how much I search for him it won't do any good. I will wait here and not stir. As long as I stay still, he in his wanderings will surely come to me. The motionless star and the moving star will meet.

JITSUKO

What if he is also waiting and not moving?

HANAKO

You don't know men.

JITSUKO

Hanako, please don't be unreasonable. I beg of you.

HANAKO

Oh, I'm so tired. You haven't any consideration for how tired I am, have you, Jitsuko? Every day I must sit on a hard wooden bench waiting for him. Day after day. I am tired. I don't look it perhaps. I suppose that I look like a big, glossy rose. But I am really very tired. I'll rest for a while. It will do me good to lay my head a little on the pillow and sleep for an hour or two. Then I shall look like a little island fast asleep. Like a little island sunken in sleep while it waits, day after day, its harbor turned to the broad sea, wondering if one of the sailboats off the shore, transparent in the scarlet of the setting sun, will not head to port. Even in the day the moon appears, and even at night the sun shines. On that island there is no need for clocks. Today I shall throw away my clock.

JITSUKO

(*sadly*) Why?

HANAKO

Then the train will never leave.

(*Exit* HANAKO. JITSUKO *stands still for a moment. She looks at the scraps of paper and begins to sweep them together toward the door with a broom. She is about to throw them away when she notices a man standing in the door.*)

JITSUKO

Who is it?

YOSHIO

Is Hanako here?

JITSUKO

(*drawing herself up*) There's nobody here by that name.

YOSHIO

I'm sure that she's here. (*He produces a newspaper from his pocket.*) I read about her in this morning's newspaper.

JITSUKO

The newspapers must be going in for misinformation, as usual.

YOSHIO

(*stepping farther in*) Please let me see Hanako.

JITSUKO

(*already realizing, but asking anyway*) Who *are* you?

YOSHIO

If you say that Yoshio is here, she'll know who I am.

JITSUKO

That name has been familiar to me for a long time. A hateful name with a disagreeable ring to it.

YOSHIO

(*Remains silent.*)

JITSUKO

In the first place I have no way of knowing whether or not you are the real Yoshio.

YOSHIO

If you have any doubts, look at this. It's her fan, with moonflowers painted on it.

JITSUKO

I wonder where you could have picked it up.

YOSHIO

I thought that you would say something like that. Now, if you would be so kind as to take me to her . . .

JITSUKO

When you saw the newspaper article you suddenly fancied yourself the hero of a love story and came rushing here—wasn't that it? To a woman you had abandoned for three years.

YOSHIO

I managed things extremely badly, I know. But about a year ago I at last became free, and I went to the town where I left her. She was no longer there. People said that after she had gone out of her mind and couldn't perform any more as a geisha, her contract was bought out by a lady artist, who took her off to Tokyo. That was all I could find out. The artist was you, wasn't it?

JITSUKO

Yes, it was I, a spinster painter on the verge of forty. I went to that town about a year and a half ago on a sketching trip. The geishas were talking about her at a restaurant to which I was invited. One summer, they said, she and a young customer from Tokyo met. The man promised to come again, and exchanged fans with her by way of a pledge. Every day she would look at the fan and think of him, and her days were spent waiting for his return. She stopped performing for customers, and was so hounded by the madame that the poor thing finally lost her mind. When I heard this story I begged to see her. She sat in a room like a dark prison, her eyes cast down, clutching a fan in her small white hands, apparently unaware even when I entered. When I spoke, she at last lifted her face. The beauty of that innocent face, like the moon with a ring round it! I fell in love at first sight. I bought out Hanako's contract and returned with her to Tokyo. At the time I made a vow to myself never to let her be stolen from me by that faithless man.

YOSHIO

Since then, for the past year and a half, she's been in your hands, I take it.

JITSUKO

I'll thank you not to adopt that tone, exactly as if you had left one of your belongings in my keeping.

YOSHIO

Then you won't let me see her. . . . In other words, her happiness is not what you desire.

JITSUKO

I desire exactly what she desires, and she has no desire whatever for happiness.

YOSHIO

(*with a defiant smile*) Then, just supposing I came here in order to make her unhappy again . . .

JITSUKO

Her unhappiness is beautiful and perfect. No one can intrude.

YOSHIO

Then there is no need to be so afraid of letting me see her.

JITSUKO

Afraid? Yes, I value my good fortune.

YOSHIO

At last you've come out with the truth.

JITSUKO

You have no comprehension of what my good fortune is. I am a woman who has never been loved by anyone, even when I was a child. I never have waited for anything. To this day I have always been alone. And that is not the worst. If by a remote chance someone were to love me, I have come to think that I would probably hate him in return. I can't allow any man to love me. . . . That was why I began my life of dreaming—dreaming of making a captive of someone who was very deeply in love, but not with me. What do you think of that? Someone who would live, most beautifully, in place of me, my helpless love. As long as that person's love is unrequited, the heart is mine.

YOSHIO

Is that what your good fortune involves?

JITSUKO

Yes.

YOSHIO

People who aren't loved think up horrible things, don't they?

JITSUKO

All love is horrible, and there are no rules. Even a love as free of pain as yours some day will experience the same horror. I like each day to light a flame of hope on the all but extinguished wick of her faint desires. But do not expect me to have hopes of my own.

YOSHIO

One thing clear to me at any rate is that you and I are enemies. Well, then, what do you give her? Is it hope? By making a decoy of me? That would seem to be all. I think that I can give her the world.

JITSUKO

You lie. All you can do is to steal the world from her. Her world has come in pieces, and it would amount only to being tied to you—a stupid and, what's more, deceitful husband.

YOSHIO

That may be, for all I care. You can't tell unless you've tried.

JITSUKO

I won't let her be tried any further. She is a flawless, inviolable gem. A deranged gem. There must be someone more suitable for worthless rubble like you.

YOSHIO

Say it plainly. You're afraid to let me see her.

JITSUKO

You don't know, do you, what stratagems an unloved woman will go to so as not to be left alone? You are obviously a person who has never once been alone.

YOSHIO

Come now, take me to Hanako.

JITSUKO

As a special favor, please don't shout.

YOSHIO

If you don't take me to her, I'll go myself.

JITSUKO

Youth, passion—in fact, a complete set of equipment to put in your pocket, and the confidence that any lock can be opened. I'm no match for you. Do you see the suitcases? I was just thinking that we would have to go off on a journey somewhere to escape from you.

YOSHIO

Does Hanako want to go away?

JITSUKO

No. She was acting peevish and went off to have a nap.

YOSHIO

She still has her wits about her.

JITSUKO

No, it is a sign of her madness.

YOSHIO

You certainly try your best to make Hanako out to be insane. I suppose that suits your convenience.

JITSUKO

I have only known Hanako since she lost her mind. That has made her supremely beautiful. The commonplace dreams she had when she was sane have now been completely purified and have become precious, strange jewels that lie beyond your comprehension.

YOSHIO

Say what you will, flesh is in those dreams.

JITSUKO

Flesh! please do not make me think of things that are distasteful to me.

YOSHIO

I am not trying to make you think of anything.

JITSUKO

(*suddenly intense*) Please go at once.

YOSHIO

What new suggestion is this after all we've gone over?

JITSUKO

I am afraid. I am afraid.

YOSHIO

I can well understand that you would be.

JITSUKO

Just supposing she should return to her senses . . .

YOSHIO

Compared to you any madman is in his senses.

JITSUKO

If she should go off and abandon me . . .

YOSHIO

I will make her abandon you.

JITSUKO

I shall die.

YOSHIO

You—die? I don't think that will make Hanako unhappy. Now if I were to die . . .

JITSUKO

You think Hanako would be stricken with grief? No—that would be the best thing you could do. Please do die. That will give her a reason to go on living.

YOSHIO

Which will give you a reason for living. No, thank you kindly. (*He goes toward the bedroom.*)

JITSUKO

Don't go there!

YOSHIO

Hanako, I've come!

JITSUKO

Go away, please. After killing me.

YOSHIO

Hanako! Hanako!

JITSUKO

(*crouching before him*) Go away, go away.

YOSHIO

(*softly, sidestepping her*) Hanako! Here's the fan. The fan with the moonflowers. (*He opens the fan and goes toward the bedroom door.*)

JITSUKO

Oh-h-h! (*She cowers on the floor, hiding her face.*)

(*The door of the bedroom opens and* HANAKO *appears. She holds against her breast the fan with the snow scene. A long pause.* HANAKO *slowly approaches* YOSHIO.)

YOSHIO

It's I, Yoshio. I've kept you waiting for me such a long time, I know. I'm sorry, Hanako. I've taken good care of your fan.

HANAKO

My . . . fan . . .

YOSHIO

Yes, with the moonflowers on it. And that fan you have with the snow scene is mine.

HANAKO

My fan . . . your fan. What happened to the fan? Were you looking for a fan?

YOSHIO

No. For you. For Hanako.

HANAKO

I . . . the fan . . .

YOSHIO

Don't you understand me? Hanako! (*He places his hand on her shoulder and shakes her. As he does so* JITSUKO, *having recovered her strength, stands motionless and stares at them.*)

HANAKO

Yoshio?

YOSHIO

Yes, I am Yoshio.

HANAKO

(*A long pause. She shakes her head almost imperceptibly.*) No you are not. You are not.

YOSHIO

What are you saying? Have you forgotten me?

HANAKO

You look very much like him. Your face is exactly like his, just as I've seen it in dreams. And yet you are different. The faces of all the men in the world are dead, and only Yoshio's face was alive. You are not Yoshio. Your face is dead.

YOSHIO

What!

HANAKO

You too are a skeleton. Your face is only bones. Why do you look at me that way with your hollow eyes of bone?

YOSHIO

Look steadily. Look at me steadily.

HANAKO

I am looking. I am looking more steadily than you. (*to* JITSUKO) Jitsuko, you're trying to deceive me again, aren't you? To deceive me and take me away with you on a trip against my wishes. You sent for this total stranger and got him to say that he was Yoshio. You're trying to make me give up the idea of waiting, yesterday, today, tomorrow, waiting the same way—aren't you? But I won't give it up. I'll wait longer. I still have in me the strength to wait a long, long time. I am alive. I can tell a dead man's face as soon as I see one.

JITSUKO

(*to* YOSHIO, *gently*) Please go. You had best resign yourself to it.

YOSHIO

(*longingly*) Hanako!
(HANAKO, *without turning back, walks to an easy-chair where she sits, facing the audience.* YOSHIO *watches her. A long pause.* YOSHIO *suddenly rushes out.*)

HANAKO

Come here.

JITSUKO

Yes.

(*It begins to grow dark outside.*)

HANAKO

It's evening already, isn't it?

JITSUKO

Yes.

HANAKO

In the evening the morning sun shines and the cocks crow, don't they? On an island you don't need a clock.

JITSUKO

Yes.

HANAKO

Jitsuko, why do we have to go away?

JITSUKO

We don't have to go any more. We'll stay here always.

HANAKO

Will we? Oh, I'm so glad. . . . Jitsuko—

JITSUKO

Yes?

HANAKO

That man who came here before. Who was he?

JITSUKO

Did someone come?

HANAKO

Yes, I'm sure someone came. He had some business, I think.

JITSUKO

Yes.

HANAKO

He was saying something in a loud voice. I hate people who talk in such loud voices.

JITSUKO

Yes, I hate them too.

HANAKO

(*She is playing with the fan again.*) That's what waiting is. . . . Waiting, waiting . . . and soon the day ends.

JITSUKO

You wait. I'm not waiting for anything.

HANAKO

I wait.

JITSUKO

I wait for nothing.

HANAKO

I wait . . . and today has grown dark too.

JITSUKO

(*her eyes flashing*) Oh, wonderful life!

CURTAIN

❁ *BIBLIOGRAPHICAL NOTE*

❁ *FOUR* of the original Nō plays on which Mr. Mishima's versions are based have been translated into English. They are SOTOBA KOMACHI, KANTAN, THE DAMASK DRUM, and THE LADY AOI. HANJO has never been translated in its entirety. All four of the translated plays may be found in Arthur Waley's excellent *The Nō Plays of Japan* (Alfred A. Knopf, New York, 1922; Grove Press, New York, 1953). (Here THE LADY AOI is called AOI NO UYE, following the original.)

Another translation of the original SOTOBA KOMACHI, by Sam Houston Brock, may be found in my *Anthology of Japanese Literature* (Grove Press, New York, 1955), which also contains some critical essays by Zeami.

The best introduction to the Nō in a Western language is *Le Nô* by Noël Peri, a book published by Maison Franco-Japonaise in Tokyo in 1944. For a discussion of the Nō as it fits into the historical development of the theater in Japan, the reader should consult *Japanese Theatre* by Faubion Bowers (Thomas Nelson & Sons, New York, 1952).

DONALD KEENE

❀ *ABOUT THE AUTHOR*

❀ *ON NOVEMBER* 25, 1970, Yukio Mishima committed *seppuku* (ritual suicide). Forty-five years old and at the peak of a brilliant literary career, he had that morning written the last word of the final novel of his tetralogy, *The Sea of Fertility*. "The tetralogy is his masterpiece, as he knew," Donald Keene has said.

Mishima had written much about suicide and early death, and often told his friends he wished to die young. After he conceived the idea of *The Sea of Fertility* in 1964, he frequently said he would die when it was completed. In fact the second of the four novels, *Runaway Horses,* is a remarkable literary rehearsal of his *seppuku*. Just before his suicide, he wrote his closest friends that he felt empty, having put into the tetralogy everything he thought and felt about life and this world. "The title, *The Sea of Fertility*," he told Keene, "is intended to suggest the arid sea of the moon that belies its name. Or I might say that it superimposes the image of cosmic nihilism on that of the fertile sea."

Mishima's works have been compared to the works of Proust, Gide, and Sartre, and his obsession with courage and the manly virtues has been likened to Hemingway's. Arthur Miller said, "I felt Mishima had an admirable style. He was surrealistic. He was very erotic. He had an economy of means to create enormous myths —his novels are compressed visions." A British magazine called him "one of the outstanding modern writers of fiction, possessing a complex, subtle and frightening imaginative power."

He was often wrongly called a rightist because of his private "army" of a hundred unarmed young men, but it was not on the blacklist of the careful Japanese police because it had never been involved in violence and differed from conventional rightist organizations. It was a theatrical fantasy conceived by a poet, as was his death, about which Selig Harrison of the Washington *Post* wrote, "He forced the Japanese to consider where they are going more dramatically than anyone else since World War II, and he has done so with a distinctively Japanese symbolism."

Mishima was born into a samurai family and imbued with the code that apotheosized complete control over mind and body, and loyalty to the Emperor—the same code that produced the austerity and self-sacrifice of Zen. Much of the tetralogy shows that he viewed the self-seeking arrogance and corruption of the militarists of the thirties (and their contemporary successors) as inimical to the samurai code.

His first novel was published in his school magazine when he was thirteen. A perceptive teacher encouraged him and persuaded a magazine to publish a story, *The Forest in Full Bloom,* in 1941, when Mishima (a pen name the teacher suggested) was sixteen. Three years later, when he entered Tokyo Imperial University, his first collection of stories was published under the same title and pen name. The first printing sold out in a week. In 1946 he brought two essays in manuscript to Kawabata, later the Nobel Prize winner, whose protégé he became. Altogether, 257 books by him, including 15 novels, have been published in Japan, and 77 translations here and in Europe.

Mishima reverenced and mastered the martial arts of Japan, creating a beautiful body he hoped age would never make ugly. He began to practice body-building in 1955, and *kendo* (dueling with bamboo staves) in 1959. In 1966 he took up *karate* as well. By 1968 he had become a *kendo* master of the fifth rank.

He traveled widely and often, and two travel books and many collections of articles are among his works. He also wrote countless short stories and thirty-three plays, in some of which he acted. Some ten films have been made from his novels; *The Sound of Waves* (1954, American edition 1956) was filmed twice, and one of the director Ichikawa's masterpieces, *Enjo,* was based on *The Temple of the Golden Pavilion* (1956, American edition 1959). Also available in English are the novels *After the Banquet* (1960, American edition 1963), *The Sailor Who Fell from Grace with the Sea* (1963, American edition, 1965), *Forbidden Colors* (1951, American edition 1968), *Thirst for Love* (1950, American edition 1969), and *Spring Snow* (1968, American edition 1972).

❁ *ABOUT THE TRANSLATOR*

❁ *DONALD KEENE* was born in New York City in 1922. He was educated at Columbia, Harvard, and Cambridge universities. From 1948 to 1953 he taught at Cambridge, after which he spent two years in Japan as a Ford Fellow. Since 1955 he has been Professor of Japanese at Columbia. His published works include two anthologies of Japanese literature, a general introduction to the subject, studies of Japanese literary and historical themes, and a translation of *After the Banquet,* a novel by Yukio Mishima.